Praise for *Growing Up Social*

Whether you are a parent, grandparent, neighbor, or friend, *Growing Up Social* is a must-read! The electronic age has brought us the amazing miracles of television and computer technology, but it has also brought risks to the social and intellectual development of our children. This book will inform you, and perhaps even alarm you, but then it will show you how children can enjoy screens without becoming addicted to them.

—MEL CHEATHAM, MD, clinical professor of neurosurgery

As a mom of six children, I see now more than ever how important real connections with real people are. For those of us who grew up with corded phones and letter writing pen-pals, it's easy to worry about how the screen-driven world impacts our children. Thankfully Arlene Pellicane and Dr. Gary Chapman have provided sound advice for parents in how to train children in important relational skills, while setting realistic boundaries for electronic entertainment. Need help in teaching your children communication, care, and empathy for others? This is the book you've been looking for! Great research, sound advice, and steps to success—what could be better than that?

—TRICIA GOYER, *USA Today* bestselling author of 40 books, including *Lead Your Family Like Jesus*

The advent of the digital world is a technology that has created an enormous challenge for parents. It is causing our children to spend more time in front of a computer screen or smartphone than in healthy social contact, and the consequences on children's emotional health is frightening. Research here is very clear: we are rewiring the human brain in ways that will have long-term detrimental effects.

Growing Up Social is absolutely correct in its identification of the risks facing our children. It offers practical guidance and scientifically validated techniques for protecting them from the damaging consequences of prolonged digital engagement. It has my full recommendation.

—ARCHIBALD D. HART, author of *The Digital Invasion: How Technology is Shaping You and Your Relationships*

How do you raise children thoughtfully in a screen-centric world? It's one of the most urgent questions of our time, and *Growing Up Social* is a full of smart, practical answers. Any parent seeking to nurture their family's spiritual life in this connected age, no matter their faith or philosophy, will benefit from reading it.

—WILLIAM POWERS, author, *Hamlet's BlackBerry*

It's not too late! You can rescue your children from their technology and help them learn why and how to be social. Without social skills, they'll be miserable, lonely, confused, angry, misled, depressed, unfulfilled. You know it's a huge issue today and I'm glad you're concerned. In *Growing Up Social*, Chapman and Pellicane share ideas that will equip you to have instructive conversations with your kids and make realistic and significant changes so they willingly decrease their screen time and confidently increase their friend time.

—KATHY KOCH, founder and president of Celebrate Kids, Inc., and author of *Finding Authentic Hope and Wholeness* and *How Am I Smart?* and coauthor of *No More Perfect Kids*

If you think your child is immune to an overdependence on screens, think again. Written by my trusted friends Gary Chapman and Arlene Pellicane this book is a reality pill that many modern day parents need to swallow.

—DR. KEVIN LEMAN, *New York Times* bestselling author of *Have a Happy Family by Friday*

Finally a book that educates on the very real effects screen time has on our children and daily home life. *Growing Up Social* is packed with practical wisdom and brilliant suggestions to effectively and intentionally pull families trapped in isolation away from their screens to reestablish God intended family time! Gary and Arlene, count me a raving fan of this much needed guide book for parents!

—**TRACEY EYSTER,** founder of FamilyLife's MomLifeToday.com, author of *Be the Mom* and *Beautiful Mess*

A timely and practical book that tackles one of parenting's biggest dilemma: how do we navigate this new world of technology? This book will equip parents to confidently set boundaries and create an atmosphere that uses technology in a healthy way.

—**TED CUNNINGHAM,** pastor and author of several books including *Trophy Child*

This book will help parents navigate the slippery slope of electronics in a way that emphasizes family bonding, social relating, and maintaining a healthy balance of electronic and non-electronic activities. A most welcome addition to the library of any intentional parent.

—**TODD CARTMELL,** child psychologist and author of *Project Dad* and *Raising Flexible Kids*

In this unprecedented age of technology and its accessibility, I cannot think of a more needed or more important resource for parents than *Growing Up Social.* While this book recognizes the positive contributions of technology, it serves as an important handbook for educating parents on the effects of too much screen time in our lives. It offers creative alternatives and encouragement to take back our home from the digital invasion and I highly recommend it!

—**KRISTEN WELCH,** author of *Rhinestone Jesus* and blogger at *We Are THAT Family*

As a mom, I have often felt outnumbered in my own home:
Laptop, iPod, smartphone, Xbox, tablet: 5 vs. Mom and Dad: 2
Besides living in a wireless bunker, what's a parent to do? *Growing Up Social* will help you reclaim your home and your family. More than a media manifesto, this book gives a commonsense, real world approach to building relationships and helping our kids who are screen savvy become socially savvy.

—**KATHI LIPP,** author of *I Need Some Help Here: Hope for When Your Kids Don't Go According to Plan* and *21 Ways to Connect with Your Kids*

Growing Up Social is a must-read for wisdom to maximize the positives and minimize the negatives of life and love in the ever-changing digital world.

—**PAM AND BILL FARREL,** co-directors of Love-Wise; authors of *Men Are Like Waffles, Women Are Like Spaghetti* and *10 Best Decisions a Parent Can Make*

Imagine this: A two-year-old picks up his mother's phone and swipes his finger across the screen. Not hard to imagine, is it? What's wrong with that picture? What's right? Arlene Pellicane and Dr. Gary Chapman will help you answer both of those questions. *Growing Up Social* is a must-read for today's parents and grandparents too!

—**KENDRA SMILEY,** author of *Journey of a Strong-Willed Child* and *Be the Parent* (and mother of three, grandmother of nine and counting)

growing up social

raising relational kids
in a screen-driven world

GARY CHAPMAN
ARLENE PELLICANE

NORTHFIELD PUBLISHING

CHICAGO

Scriptures taken from the Holy Bible, New International Version®, NIV®. Copyright © 1973, 1978, 1984, 2011 by Biblica, Inc. Used by permission of Zondervan. All rights reserved worldwide. www.zondervan.com. The "NIV" and "New International Version" are trademarks registered in the United States Patent and Trademark Office by Biblica, Inc.

Scripture quotations marked THE MESSAGE are from *The Message,* copyright © by Eugene H. Peterson 1993, 1994, 1995. Used by permission of NavPress Publishing Group.

Edited by Annette LaPlaca
Cover design: Brand Navigation
Cover photo of children at table copyright © 2013 by Andrew Rich/iStock. All rights reserved.
Interior design: Smartt Guys design
Gary Chapman photo: P.S. Photography
Arlene Pellicane photo: Anthony Amorteguy

All websites and phone numbers listed herein are accurate at the time of publication, but may change in the future or cease to exist. The listing of website references and resources does not imply publisher endorsement of the site's entire contents. Groups and organizations are listed for informational purposes, and listing does not imply publisher endorsement of their activities.

Library of Congress Cataloging-in-Publication Data

Chapman, Gary D.
Growing up social : raising relational kids in a screen-driven world /
Gary D Chapman, Arlene Pellicane.
    pages cm
Includes bibliographical references.
ISBN 978-0-8024-1123-5 (paperback)
1. Internet and children. 2. Parenting. 3. Families. I. Pellicane, Arlene, 1971- II. Title.
HQ784.I58C43 2014
004.67'8083--dc23
                    2014011371

We hope you enjoy this book from Northfield Publishing. Our goal is to provide high-quality, thought-provoking books and products that connect truth to your real needs and challenges. For more information on other books and products written and produced from a biblical perspective, go to www.moodypublishers.com or write to:

Northfield Publishing
820 N. LaSalle Boulevard
Chicago, IL 60610

1 3 5 7 9 10 8 6 4 2

Printed in the United States of America

contents

"*We can be a home on a hill, shining in the lonely darkness.*"

—DR. DAVID JEREMIAH, *GIFTS FROM GOD*

taking back
your home

I s technology bringing your family closer together, or is it driving your family farther apart?

Joseph and Amanda have three children, ages two, six, and ten. Their kids play video games and watch movies and television all day except for the time the older kids are in school. Joseph and Amanda are concerned about the amount of time their children spend in front of screens, yet they feel powerless to make a change.

"We have no guidelines," said Joseph. "We did have guidelines but could not keep them in place."

Can you identify with these discouraged parents? Maybe you've tried to limit screen time in the past, but the temper tantrums were too much to bear. We've heard from hundreds of parents who express their frustration with implementing digital guidelines:

"We have no rules. Our kids watch a lot of TV and play video games."

"Screen time rules aren't stated; they're implied, and it's not working."

"I regret not having guidelines because my son missed out on socializing with people face to face. He's in his twenties and completely engrossed with being on his computer."

You want your adult child to have all the skills necessary to succeed in relationships. The training necessary for growing up social isn't found on a phone or tablet. There's no app or video game that can replace interactions with other human beings. Social skills must be practiced in real life, beginning for a child in the home.

Having a social child means your son or daughter will be able to talk to people and like people. He'll be able to relate to others and enjoy activities with friends and family members. Being social isn't just about making small talk in the cafeteria. It involves showing other people you care through eye contact, conversation, and empathy. The ideal place for a child to learn to be social is in his home, where a loving mother or father can model what healthy relationships look like.

Unfortunately, there is a subtle shift happening in many homes that is profoundly eroding the relationship between parent and child. The average American child and teenager spends fifty-three hours a week with media and technology, far more time in front of screens than interacting with parents or people.[1] How is a growing child supposed to learn about getting along with others when the vast majority of her time is spent with a screen?

average isn't working

Teenagers aren't the only demographic prone to peer pressure. Parents are just as quick to get their child the latest digital device to keep up with the family across the street. The other fourth graders have cellphones, so you get your daughter one too. If the other kids are playing a particular violent video game, what's the harm in your son joining in? You wouldn't want him to feel left out! Or maybe you feel bad about plunking your toddler in front of the screen for a few hours each day, but at least all the other kids are watching the same programs.

It doesn't take much effort to join the digital crowd and entertain your children with what makes them happy (and quiet). We surveyed hundreds of parents about their families and screens. Many reported that screens ran their children's lives, yet they were not concerned. One parent said, "My children can watch as much as they want, usually four to five hours a day. I am not concerned, and I don't think it's affected our family dynamic."

The presence of screens in the home is so widely accepted that many parents don't even consider them a threat to strong family relationships. Let us take a moment to assure you that this is not an antitechnology book. Technology is here to stay, and we believe you can find positive ways to utilize it for your relationships. No doubt your child is going to use emails, texts, and smartphones as he grows into an adult. These are amazing days when you can videoconference Grandma in a different country in real time. But if you don't minimize and monitor the screens in your child's life, when your son finally meets Grandma face to face, he may not know how to simply sit and visit.

Screens are not the problem; the problem lies in the way we constantly use them. When your child has free time, what's his default activity? For the average family, free time equals screen time. It's one experience to gather around the television to watch a DVD with your family. This is intentional screen time that can bring a family closer. It's another experience to click through channels mindlessly day after day. Screen time that is not purposeful tends to be a waste of time and negative influence.

If the average family is glued to screens, texts instead of talks, and uses phones while eating together at restaurants, who wants to be average? The digital norm does not appear to be producing healthy, relationally rich children. Screens aren't anything new; parents may have watched a lot of television while growing up. But our televisions were big and bulky, fixed on a piece of furniture. Phone calls were limited to the house because the phone was strapped to the wall or you couldn't get reception past the garage on a cordless.

Today we carry screens *in our pockets* wherever we go. Screens have moved out of the background into the foreground—for adults and for children as well. Pixels instead of people take center stage for the average American family. Children are like wet cement, and nowadays most are being imprinted by screens, not by parents.

It doesn't have to be this way.

no more good intentions

Many well-intentioned parents say things like:

"Life is busy; I don't have time to enforce screen-time rules."

"I couldn't get my spouse to back up what I was doing."

"My kids threw a fit when I tried to make a change."

"It's so hard to be consistent."

Nina has three daughters, ages two, four, and six. The girls were watching five hours of cartoons every day. Dinner was centered on the television, and Nina knew the lack of family time wasn't good. She attempted to turn off the television for mealtimes and in the early evening.

But after only a few nights of success, life got especially busy and Nina pretended not to notice when the girls turned on the television after dinner. Before long, the girls were back on the couch, watching television on most evenings.

Good intentions will not get you anywhere as a parent. Author Andy Andrews writes,

> Despite popular belief to the contrary, there is absolutely no power in intention. The seagull may intend to fly away, may decide to do so, may talk with the other seagulls about how wonderful it is to fly, but until the seagull flaps his wings and takes to the air, he is still on the dock.

There's no difference between that gull and all the others. Likewise, there is no difference in the person who intends to do things differently and the one who never thinks about it in the first place. Have you ever considered how often we judge ourselves by our intentions while we judge others by their actions? Yet intention without action is an insult to those who expect the best from you.[2]

We share these powerful and convicting words about the difference between good intentions and actions to appeal to you to read this book for ideas you will *use*. We don't expect you to agree with every idea presented in *Growing Up Social*. But we hope you will take the ideas that resonate with you and put them into practice.

No matter how smart screens get, your child's natural curiosity is best matched with a caring parent who will help him understand his world. Let's go back to the question we started with: *Is technology bringing your family closer together, or is it driving your family farther apart?* Believe it or not, you can make positive changes that will influence your child for the rest of his life. The journey to taking back your home from screens starts now.

"The more a child is involved in screen time, the less time there is for interaction with parents, siblings, and friends." —DR. GARY CHAPMAN

screen time:
too much, too soon?

Fifteen-month-old Lily sits in the shopping cart, eyes fixed on her iPad. Her mom shops along the grocery store aisle with minimal interruptions. Lily never looks up to see the bright red apples or the shelf where her beloved Cheerios are grandly displayed.

Every weekday, third grader Jason flips on the television after school. The TV stays on for five hours until he goes to bed.

Melissa is a junior in high school. Last month, she sent 3,500 text messages (that's about 110 texts per day).

These are not unusual scenarios. They have become the norm in a child's screen-driven world. No wonder parents consider how to balance the use of technology with everyday life. Moms, dads, and grandparents are asking, "Dr. Chapman, my children are on the phone or playing video games constantly. We don't have family time anymore. When we tell them we're going to do something as a family, they argue and head back to their screens."

Remember what life was like before smartphones, flat screens, and tablets? Before the digital age, children went out in the yard and played, creating their own games or engaging in endless rounds of freeze tag or hide-and-seek. Kids learned to interact. They had to deal with winning and losing, getting kicked by a neighbor, and being empathetic to a friend who got hurt. Boys and girls learned how the real world works through playing with one another. Yet most children today are indoors for the bulk of their free time. Children aren't allowed to roam outside as they once were because of the fear of kidnapping and other societal dangers. So they stay indoors, often engaged with a screen instead of a person. Unfortunately, the more a child is involved in screen time, the less time there is for interaction with parents, siblings, and friends.

plugged in too soon?
screen time for children under two

The temptation to use screens to entertain babies and toddlers is stronger than ever. With our homes, vehicles, and smartphones, we are surrounded by media. Not only are screens ever-present, a parent almost feels *obligated* to utilize the latest, greatest educational software.

But research and our personal experience say the less exposure your little one has to screens, the better. The American Academy of Pediatrics (AAP) recommends that parents avoid television viewing and screen time for children under the age of two.[1] The AAP believes the negative effects of media use far outweigh the positive ones for this age group. Despite the luminous claims of educational videos and software, little evidence supports educational or developmental benefits from media use by children younger than two years. You'd never know that, based on the glut of electronic educational products geared toward making smart babies and toddlers!

Young children grow by discovering the world. They need to experience a three-dimensional world of people and things they can taste, touch, see, hear, and smell. This foundational exploration can't happen if a baby or toddler spends a lot of time using electronics. Children are walking at two, which means they are going to get into trouble—that's normal and healthy. They learn which doors are okay to open and which doors stay shut. They're developing motor skills as they walk up and down stairs. During this important developmental stage, screen time hinders more than it helps.

The AAP actually reports adverse health effects of direct media use as well as parental media use (background media) in the life of a young child. Because of their early stage of cognitive development, children under two years of age process information differently from older children. Two studies have found that watching a program like *Sesame Street* has a negative—not positive—effect on language development for children younger than two years.[2] While you may think a television show or phone app is teaching your baby the ABCs, media use has not been proven to promote language skills in little ones. Young children learn language best when it's presented by a live person and not on a screen.

A study from 2007 reported that 90 percent of parents allow their children younger than two years to watch some form of electronic media.[3] Thirty-nine percent of families with infants and young children have a television on at least six hours per day[4]—with negative effects. Studies show that while television may be background noise for the child, it often moves to the foreground for the parent. A child's ability to learn language is directly related to the amount of talk time he or she has with a parent. When the television is on, Mom or Dad is less likely to engage in conversation, resulting in a smaller vocabulary for that child.

Researchers examined twelve-, twenty-four-, and thirty-six-month-olds and found that background television not only reduced the length of time a child played, but it also reduced the child's focused attention during play.[5] Other studies suggest that background media might interfere with cognitive processing, memory, and reading comprehension. In spite of these negative effects, almost one-third of children have a television in their bedroom by age three.[6] It isn't wise for any child, regardless of age, to have a television in her own room (more about that in chapter 11). Many young children use the television as a sleep aid, even though television viewing before falling asleep is associated with irregular sleep schedules and poor sleep habits that affect mood, behavior, and learning.

The best alternative to watching a video with your young child is cuddling up and reading a book. As your child is exposed to books, his or her vocabulary will grow. Becoming a great reader begins with listening, so read aloud and often to your son or daughter.

What if you've allowed your young child to watch television, but now you want to pull back? Melissa, a mother of children ages two and four, wants to do the right thing for her children's development, but she wonders how to get dinner on the table without the help of the television to keep her kids occupied. On the next page are a few ideas to help replace screen time with project time.

It takes effort to switch from the convenience of screen time to an interactive or tactile activity for a child. But the benefits for your son's or daughter's development are well worth it. You will be pleasantly surprised at how quickly your child adjusts to new screen-free routines.

plugged in too much?

Eight-year-old Trevor asked the question for the hundredth time, "Mom, all my friends have a video game player. Why won't you let me get one?"

"Just because all your friends have one doesn't mean it's a good idea for you," answered his mom.

Although Donna had been able to ward off her son's request for two years, she began to wonder if it might be the right time to say yes. After all, Trevor was a good student. She decided to surprise him with a video game console for Christmas.

Scribbling. Place big pieces of butcher paper on the floor and give your child a box of crayons. An eighteen-month-old can hold a crayon and scribble. Scribbling helps your toddler to develop a tripod position of the hand for drawing and writing, a needed skill your child will not learn from swiping a screen.

Cardboard Box. Keep a large cardboard box your toddler can climb in and out of. Add some crayons if your child wants to decorate it.

Special Cupboard. Fill a cupboard your child can reach with plastic cups and plates, measuring cups, spoons, and bowls. This could also be your Tupperware cupboard. Let your child use this cupboard only when you're making meals to make it a special activity when you're in the kitchen.

Water Fun. If you have a tile floor that can handle it, fill a bowl with an inch or two of water. Give your child some measuring cups or spoons along with a few toys that will float or sink.

MAGIC TOY BOX. Take a plastic bin and fill it with toys your child hasn't played with for a while. Give her the bin with great fanfare. Change the contents every week to add an element of surprise. Your child will actually play with these toys instead of letting them go to waste.

Jumping Beans. This one is messier, but give your child a large pan filled with dry beans, measuring cups, and funnels. Put out a cookie sheet so your child can make designs with the beans.

It didn't take long for Trevor to adapt to having his own gaming system at his fingertips. During most of his free time, he played video games. On the car ride home from school, he gave short answers to his mom's questions about the day, all the while playing his video game. Donna began to wonder if she had made a mistake.

"I didn't realize it would take away so much of his time," Donna said. "Now when I ask him to put it away, we get in an argument. It's hard for him to stop playing for dinnertime or to practice his piano. I regret giving it to him without setting guidelines from the start."

Trevor isn't the only one glued to his electronic device. The average American child age eight to age eighteen spends more than seven hours per day looking at a video game, computer, cellphone, or television.[7] By the age of seven, a child born today will have spent one full year of twenty-four-hour days watching screen media.[8]

The frequent use of video games by children is particularly concerning because of the possibility of addiction. Video games are designed to bring pleasure to the brain. Players accumulate points, get constant rewards, and reach higher levels. Visually, the video game changes constantly to reengage your child. While playing, the brain rewards the child with a squirt of dopamine, providing a feeling of euphoria (more on this subject in chapter 9). The more you play, the more you want to play.

The symptoms of video game addiction are similar to those of addictions to alcohol, drugs, or gambling. Video games begin interfering with everyday life. Personal hygiene isn't practiced. Assignments, chores, and responsibilities are left undone. Family relationships suffer. Nothing is quite as stimulating or rewarding as playing video games.

For Michael, a senior in high school, video games were his life. His parents hosted a graduation party to honor him. During that celebration with family and friends, Michael lasted about ten minutes before he retreated to his room alone, shut the door, and began playing video games. No one could coax him out of his room. Within an hour, everyone had left the party.

Although extreme, Michael's story illustrates what can happen when boys are raised by video games and the Internet. In their twenties, they remain in a prolonged adolescence that prevents them from going out into the real world to find jobs, to socialize, and to become independent.

Excessive screen time isn't only a problem for boys. Girls watch television just as much as boys do. Girls in neighborhoods ranked as the lowest third by socioeconomic factors are five times more likely to watch the highest amount of screen time.[9] High school girls average 4,300 texts a month, while boys trail behind at 2,600 texts a month.[10]

So how much daily screen time is too much for your family? The AAP recommends that children older than two years old should get no more than two hours a day of screen time.[11] This means if your child is on the computer for one hour at school, they should only have one additional hour at home. With more elementary schools incorporating iPads into the classroom, it's even more important (and challenging) to limit screen time at home. Children need unplugged time to unwind, read, play outside, and talk with parents and siblings.

In terms of how much screen time you allow your child, only you can decide how much is too much. Two hours a day is a good general rule. For many parents, that may not seem feasible. For others, two hours of screen time would be too much. Although each family should use personal judgment on the amount of screen time, every family must set clear boundaries. Children always do better if they have clear boundaries. Screen time requires time limits and parameters, or it will take over your child's free time.

My First Smartphone and Lucy

Believe it or not, I (Arlene) got my first smartphone right before I started writing this book. Why did I hold on to my dinosaur phone for so long? Since I already spend hours on my personal computer at home, I didn't see the need to have my emails and social networking sites handy at all times. But as I started traveling more, I realized a smartphone would be a smart move. Reluctantly, I made the switch.

At first I was enamored. I checked my phone constantly, several times per hour. Did I get a new email? Let me post a picture on Facebook. Who just messaged me? It was ridiculous. I quickly realized I needed to put it down or suffer the consequences of constant distraction. I made a decision to reach for it a few times per day to check it.

Then there was the matter of my four-year-old, Lucy. From time with her friends, she had seen what the little phone could do. She gravitated to it instantly, using her little fingers to push the colorful apps. In a flash of brilliance, I told her, "Lucy, that is Mommy's phone. It is not yours. It's a 'no touch.' If we are in an airplane, I will let you use it." I had not premeditated that response but realized in that moment if the phone became fair game for Lucy, she would ask for it constantly. That was one daily struggle I didn't want to sign up for.

Lucy thought for a moment then said, "I was in an airplane last month to visit Grandma." I laughed and replied, "I know. I didn't have the phone then."

Lucy never touches my phone, although believe me, she is itching to use that camera. The phone sits on my desk, powerless to weave its magic spell on my four-year-old. Making my phone off-limits to Lucy was one of my best tech decisions. Now it's reserved for emergency moments. Plus, it may not be wise to give a four-year-old a "toy" that costs several hundred dollars. Of course, Lucy is really looking forward to her next airplane ride.

plugged in to what?

When my (Gary's) children were little, we didn't have computers, but we did have television. We chose about five programs that were appropriate for our kids to watch. We told them, "You can have thirty minutes a day and watch any one of these programs." This way, our children developed the ability to make decisions within healthy parameters that we set as parents. Both lessons are important: to teach children to make decisions and to teach them to live within boundaries.

The television set of the past used to be a large piece of furniture, planted smack-dab in the middle of the living room and family life. Parents knew which shows were good for kids and which weren't. As gatekeepers, they were in full control of every program being watched in the home. Then televisions became more compact and affordable. Families began having more than one television set, making it more difficult to monitor what children were watching.

Fast-forward to today: Technology has given us instant information and entertainment on televisions, personal computers, tablets, and smartphones. We no longer have one television to gather around as a family. The family television of the past is now multiplied in every family member's pocket, purse, or backpack. And even though television wasn't necessarily wholesome then, it's certainly more vulgar, sexual, and violent now.

When your child has easy access to a television or the Internet, a whole world of inappropriate content is waiting to be consumed. I (Arlene) remember going to see the Superman movie *Man of Steel* with my husband. The movie was rated PG-13 for "intense sequences of sci-fi violence, action and destruction, and for some language." I was shocked to see how many children were in the theater seated right next to their parents. Many boys looked like they were seven or eight. There were a few five-year-olds and even some toddlers in strollers. The movie started at 8:15 p.m., and it was too late, too loud, and too intense for young children. PG and PG-13 movies come with a warning to parents for a reason. Superhero franchises appeal to young children, but make no mistake: Most of the movies are not kid-friendly. *Marvel's The Avengers*, the highest-grossing movie in 2012, had a kill count of 964 and received a PG-13 rating, "Parents strongly cautioned."[12]

There are general guidelines for deciding what content is appropriate for your child to watch. Here are four questions to help you decide whether or not it is wise for your child to view a particular program or video game:

What factual data is my child learning from this program? If there
is factual data, is it correct? You want your child's mind to be filled with

truth. If the program communicates a distorted vision of reality instead of how life works in the real world, you don't want your child watching. You want your child to be exposed to things that are real and not a distortion of reality.

What kind of character traits is this program seeking to build in my child? Is the main character someone I want my child to copy? If the humor comes from cutting others down, being rude, or showing disrespect to authority, that's a red light. Positive programs will teach your child to care for others, work hard, resolve conflict, or overcome obstacles.

How does this program treat family members? Television sitcoms often degrade men and fathers by making them lazy, fat, or stupid. What messages will your child hear about men, women, marriage, and parents? How is the family represented?

Is this program consistent with our family values? A child is running into all sorts of values during his or her early years. You can't control what your child sees outside at school or other places, but you can control what he or she is exposed to at home. What is viewed on screens should be in keeping with your family values, or it should be off-limits.

It is your job as a parent to teach your children the difference between appropriate and inappropriate content. Do not leave this task to a teacher, pastor, or counselor. In the same way you would not allow your child to eat candy bars for dinner each night, you cannot allow your child to consume screen-time junk food. You are the gatekeeper of your child's mental diet.

oh, how much you miss

My (Arlene's) family was headed to the beach with friends. Our family was in one minivan, and their family was in another. Both vans were close together as we drove down the highway. Suddenly from behind us, three motorcycles sped up and passed us. Right before our eyes, one of them popped a wheelie. One of the other motorcycles, which had two riders, took the challenge and did the same. We were watching a daredevil show from the comfort of our own minivan! Interstate 805 had never been so exciting! We followed those motorcycles for miles, hoping to see more of the show. We weren't disappointed as they popped more wheelies and finally zoomed off the exit ramp with great fanfare.

When we reached the beach, we excitedly said to our friends, "Wow, that was amazing! Could you believe those motorcycles?" The kids stared blankly at us. They had missed the whole thing. They had been watching a DVD and hadn't even noticed the motorcycles.

Another time, my family went on a whale-watching cruise. When that whale fin finally appeared out of the water, we spotted it. But dozens of children missed it. They were playing with electronic devices inside the cabin.

There is so much to be missed when you are fixated on a screen. It's not just about those special moments like seeing a whale's fin or watching motorcycles pop wheelies. It's about the everyday moments and chances to catch your child's eye and smile. Emotions have to do with relationships. They are the responses to what happens in our lives, both pleasant and unpleasant. Children must learn to process emotions, and none of that is learned in front of a screen but by interacting with parents, siblings, and other people in real time, face to face.

A world dominated by screens is a false, controlled world that revolves around pleasing your child. If your child doesn't like something on a device, he can just move on to the next thing until he finds something of interest. Kids don't have to learn to wait because gratification is instant. What does that teach your child? Real life certainly isn't characterized by endless options, drop-down menus, and constant pleasure.

Parents can miss much as well. Too much screen time robs you of teachable moments with your child, building family memories, and bonding with your child. It may be easier to allow your child hours of screen time, but have you considered the personal growth you may be missing out on as a parent?

Mandy, a mother of a six-year-old and a four-year-old, was concerned with her daughters' dependence on television. Whenever Mandy gave the five-minute warning, the girls would fuss. When the television was off, they argued and kept asking her to turn the television back on. Exasperated, Mandy would give in, even though the girls had already exceeded their time limit.

But what if Mandy had stayed consistent with her rules? While her daughters would be learning valuable lessons about obeying limits, Mandy would have grown in resolve, patience, and problem solving. When we as parents and grandparents opt for the easy route, we often cheat ourselves out of growing our own character.

is it too late to change?

It's never too late to start doing what's healthy. It's true on the individual level, and it's true in parenting. Any life can be turned around. As long as your children are living in your house, it's not too late to become more actively involved in training your children in healthy directions.

Steve and Tricia approached me after a conference with a question about their ten-year-old son. "Dr. Chapman, our son's a good kid. He's not a straight-A student, but he finishes his homework and does his best. Since he was in second grade, we've allowed him to play video games at home. He used to play for thirty minutes after school, but lately we've noticed he is playing a lot more. We catch him in his room playing after the lights are out. We both work, and we've just let it slide. Last week, we looked at the game he was playing and were shocked to see how violent it was. We want him to stop, but we don't know what to do."

Typically when our children are doing things we don't think they should be doing, we come down on them hard. We are harsh with them, rather than accepting responsibility ourselves. I suggested that Steve and Tricia talk with their son, saying something like this: "We have not done a very good job in the area of screen time and video games. We haven't been paying attention to what you have been playing. We deeply regret this. We have let you down in this area. But we're going to change things. From now on, we are going to help you decide which video games are good and which ones will harm you as you grow up. Will you forgive us for being absent when we should have been here to help you?"

Most kids will forgive parents who are willing to ask for forgiveness. Owning up to your responsibility as a parent is much more effective than accusing your child of poor decision making. In every home, there needs to be healthy communication between the parent and child that is not logistic in nature. Conversations aren't only about enforcing bedtime or coordinating school pick-up times. Interact with your child about whatever topic might come up, and screen time is certainly a hot topic that can be revisited often.

If you haven't had this kind of open communication with your child in the past, it's not too late to begin. As you decide what's healthy for your family and articulate a clear media game plan moving forward, your family will thrive within the boundaries you set.

"If we are not alert, the Information Age may stunt our growth and create a permanent puberty of the mind." —SHANE HIPPS

chapter two

the A+ method for
relational kids

Dr. Holden has been a dentist for the past twenty years. Since the advent of technology, he has seen many changes in his work with children. "When I enter the exam room, about one-fourth of the children are sitting in the chair with a cellphone or iPad," he says. "I have to get their attention away from their devices to talk with them. Their eyes do not move away from the screen when I enter the room. I have to compete with screens for their attention."

Dr. Holden does not have television screens in the waiting room or exam rooms of his pediatric dental office; he does have magazines, books, and toys like building blocks and dollhouses. But other, screen-friendly dental offices offer screen entertainment in every room, and Dr. Holden feels pressure to change in order to compete.

No question: the distraction of an iPad can be useful when a child is getting a cavity filled or during a long travel day. But do children really need *constant* entertainment? Too often children are given screens to pacify and occupy them when it's not an emergency or special occasion. Instead of learning how to live in the real world of communicating with people and occasionally feeling bored, they are given a screen world for their entertainment pleasure. More and more studies demonstrate the adverse effects of screen time on the brain and your child's social and emotional development.

In the year 2000, before mobile phones and computer apps were popular, the average person's attention span was twelve seconds. Since then, our attention span has dropped by 40 percent.[1] How are children going to learn the relational skills necessary for a successful life without the basic skill of paying attention? Immersing your kids in screens that are constantly changing, entertaining, engaging, and rewarding does not prepare them to succeed in reality.

real life doesn't work this way

Have you ever wondered:

How did kids and teenagers become so entitled?

Why can't kids or teens spell or write in complete sentences?

Why do my children complain and argue so much?

Why do I have to prompt my child every time to say please and thank you?

In previous generations, children were more respectful of parents and adults, stronger academically, and more courteous. Why the shift? Technology is not totally to blame, but its impact on the growing mind and heart of a child is undeniable. More and more children are being taught how life works from a screen instead of the real-life classrooms of responsibility, chores, and family relationships.

For instance, children face fewer personal challenges today. Technology makes everything easier for all of us. If you don't know what a word means, you just look it up on the computer instead of searching for it in a dictionary. If you don't know how to solve a multiplication problem, there's always the calculator. When you're bored, just reach for your favorite game or website for entertainment.

When my (Arlene's) kids talk about things they want, whether it's Legos or princess dresses, they say with great ease, "Just buy it on Amazon." Technology makes everything easily attainable in their minds. Anything can be bought with a click of the mouse. A tech-saturated child doesn't have the patience to do anything hard. Technology trains children to find what they need at the speed of light. The art of patience is lost.

the screen-driven child

When seven-year-old Sophia can't get her homework done because she doesn't know how to read her school library book, her mom calls the teacher. "I looked at the book Sophia brought home for class, and it's too advanced for second grade. Can you please change Sophia's reading assignment?"

Even though Sophia's mom has good intentions, she is actually shielding Sophia from the experience she needs to grow as an individual. Today's screen-driven child doesn't put up with a lot of suffering. If homework or soccer practice is too difficult, children want to quit. Unfortunately, many parents enable their children instead of helping them overcome obstacles. It's all right, even desirable, for a child to experience stress when learning a new skill. As long as that child feels secure in your love, she will thrive when challenged.

The screen-driven child enjoys constant rewards and fails to thrive when he isn't praised fast enough or often enough. After all, in video games you earn points, stars, or extra lives. You advance to new levels quickly. Your efforts are immediately rewarded.

Speaker and parent educator Dr. Kathy Koch tells the story of a four-year-old boy who used a basketball app on the phone. Every time he made a basket, the phone lit up and vibrated. Since he loved that game, his grandparents thought it would be a great idea to buy him a real basketball hoop. When the little boy shot his first real basket, he stood waiting for something to happen. Nothing happened—no lights, no vibrations. He shot another basket. Still nothing happened. Disenchanted, he grabbed the phone and continued to play basketball on the screen. He had learned that anything done right was rewarded instantly. When nothing happened with the real-life basketball hoop, he quit playing.

Children today are rewarded even if they don't perform well. It's common for sports teams to give every child a trophy. Regardless of whether your team wins or loses, you still get a trophy. All you have to do is show up, and you'll get something. What does that do to a child's motivation to achieve? He grows up with a false expectation that whatever effort he puts forth—excellent or poor—will be rewarded.

My (Arlene's) son, Ethan, played in his first basketball league when he was in the third grade. His team, the Magic, did not win one game the entire season. During a few games, the score was so lopsided they actually turned off the scoreboard. But the boys knew the score.

We can try to shield our children from losing, but Ethan learned a lot from that season with the Magic. In life, people fail and you don't always win. We want to help our kids develop a realistic approach to life. In sports, someone is going to win and someone is going to lose. Being a loser doesn't mean you're a bad person. All the heroes of the sports world have lost many more times than they have won. It's part of the learning process.

A losing experience offers an opportunity to ask important questions. "What can we learn from this? What can we do differently that would make you better at that?" There are valuable life lessons that only failure can teach your child. Screen time doesn't provide many chances to fail, but real life allows them to practice in the safety of your home.

the A+ child

When your child goes to school, what's the highest measure of success? A report card filled with *A*'s? Although academic achievement is a worthwhile goal, there's something more important than your child's academic record. What kind of human being is your child becoming?

More than straight *A*'s, strong moral character will predict your child's success as he or she grows into an adult. I (Arlene) had the chance to read to my son Ethan's third-grade class. As I sat down with William Bennett's *The Book of Virtues*, I asked the class of third graders, "What is a virtue?" Blank stares. They looked at the large book I was holding and concluded that a virtue was a collection of stories. Not one child besides Ethan could define the word *virtue*.

Kids know all sorts of things about video games, cartoons, and the latest apps. But they lack instruction about character. Virtues are behaviors that show high moral standards. Responsibility. Compassion. Persistence. Faith. There is no virtue app you can download into your child's heart and mind. Virtues are taught and caught as children observe and listen to their parents talk about what is right and what is wrong.

In the next five chapters, we will outline five A+ skills your child needs to develop in order to succeed in life and love. Don't abandon your efforts toward achieving academic *A*'s, but keep the following A+ relational skills in the forefront of your child's total education in your home.

the A+ skill of affection

After a challenging day at the office, Rachel walks into her home followed by her kids: Leah, age nine, and Charlie, age seven. She puts her things down and begins heating up items from the freezer for dinner. Charlie sits down in front of the television. Leah starts playing her favorite game on her iPad. Rachel's husband comes home and joins everyone for a quick dinner. No one is rude, but no one says please or thank you either. After the meal, Charlie resumes watching television and Leah picks up right where her video game left off. Rachel's husband works on his laptop while Rachel checks her phone for text messages.

At the end of the evening, Rachel closes her eyes to go to sleep. She's concerned because lately she doesn't feel close to anyone in her family. The kids seem more interested in watching television or playing video games than in being with her. Her husband rarely cuddles on the couch to talk anymore. What is happening to her once close-knit family?

Every family needs the ingredient of affection to thrive: eye contact, hugs, appropriate physical touching, and affirming words. Healthy children learn to give and receive proper affection from their family members. Relationships within the home that consist only of a few words and text messages fall short.

the A+ skill of appreciation

My (Arlene's) son, Ethan, had the chance of a lifetime to ride in a navy ship for the day during a friends and family cruise. I waved goodbye as my husband, Ethan, and Ethan's friend, ten-year-old Noah, drove to the dock. When Ethan returned at the end of the day, he was wearing a handsome baseball cap with the ship's name embroidered on it. Noah had bought him something from the ship's gift shop to say thank you for inviting him to come along.

Later I asked Noah's mom if she had prompted him to buy a gift. "No, we did not suggest he should buy something for Ethan. That was Noah's own decision and his spending money." Noah's mother was delighted to learn that her son, on his own, had shown appreciation to his friend.

At a young age, Noah understands the power of appreciation. When someone does something nice for you, the right response is to show gratitude. Sometimes it's easier for a child to think, "Well, I deserved that." But we as parents want to raise an appreciative child who becomes an appreciative adult, not an entitled child who becomes an entitled adult.

the A+ skill of anger management

Seven-year-old Joey and nine-year-old Kimberly have been on each other's nerves since the moment they woke up.

They fought over who would use the sink first in the bathroom. "Stop it!" Kimberly cried, which made Joey shove her even harder.

At breakfast, Kimberly continually nagged Joey: "You spilled the cereal. You're so clumsy. Your shirt doesn't match your pants."

While waiting for his mom to take them to school, Joey sat on the couch playing video games. Kimberly leaned over, getting in between Joey's face and the screen. "Get out of here!" he yelled as he pushed her away.

"Mom, Joey hit me!" screamed Kimberly.

Siblings have a special gift: they can drive each other crazy in a minute. Left alone, all those irritations can turn into misplaced anger between brothers and sisters. Anger isn't confined only to the home; it's common in playgrounds and classrooms too. Parents do their children a tremendous service when they teach them to recognize the difference between "bad" anger and "good" anger and how to deal with feelings of anger in a positive manner.

the A+ skill of apology

I (Gary) remember a time when my six-year-old son, confronted with knocking a glass off the table that now lay shattered on the floor, explained, "It did it by itself." When the wall was marked with Magic Marker, again he would say, "It did it by itself." We worked long and hard at getting him to say, "I accidentally knocked the glass off the table" and "I marked on the wall."

To this day, my wife and I will jokingly say to each other when confronted with an irresponsible action, "It did it by itself." We know that we are joking, but it feels good to place the blame on "it" rather than "me." If we want our children to grow into mature adults, we must teach them to accept responsibility for their behavior. Immature adults continue with childish behavior and tend to blame others for their mistakes instead of owning up.

Accepting responsibility for one's words and actions is the first step in learning to apologize. Typically children easily accept responsibility for their positive actions. "I ate three bites of my beans. May I have dessert?" "I got a smiley face on my paper." "I ran the fastest." These are all statements accepting responsibility for noble deeds done.

On the other hand, children are not as quick to accept responsibility for deeds that are not so noble. When is the last time you heard your child admit, "I'm sorry. I ate the cookie you told me not to eat" or "I cheated on my math homework because I didn't know how to solve the problem"? This level of apology takes far more parental guidance and effort. But the good news is the art of apology can be learned from a young age and applied throughout adulthood, giving your child a tremendous emotional advantage.

the A+ skill of attention

Four-year-old Aiden attends a weekly Mommy-and-Me music class. Twelve preschoolers sit in a circle while the teacher passes out instruments. While the other children are sitting on their mats and singing along with their instruments, Aiden gets up, puts his instrument back in the bucket, and noisily picks up a tambourine. His mother signals him back to his spot in the circle. "Aiden, sit down," she pleads. Ignoring his mother and the teacher, he grabs a different instrument and runs to another part of the classroom. Music class becomes a frustrating event for Aiden's mom and his teacher. After a few weeks, they drop out of the class.

Aiden's inability to pay attention isn't unusual. Rose, a veteran children's pastor, has seen a dramatic shift in how long children are able to pay attention in church. "Kids these days are looking for the unattainable, the amazing, the beyond-exciting!" Rose shares. "They are used to the stimulation of video games or movies. They want that next captivating thing to see. When it doesn't appear, they tune out. Most of the kids struggle with focus at church. When I ask them to get in a circle, it takes a long time because kids are so distracted. They dart around the room instead of simply getting in a circle. I can tell who has a lot of screen time at home because it correlates with poor listening skills and a need for strong guidance."

it starts now

We call these A+ skills. They are not characteristics some children are born with and some are not. They are learned abilities that seldom happen automatically. This is good news because it means instilling character in your child isn't like buying a lotto ticket. It's not left up to chance. You can make an impact on your child forever by teaching her how to:

Show **affection**
Appreciate others
Deal with **anger**
Learn to **apologize**
Pay **attention**

Maybe you have not been proactive in teaching these five A+ skills in the past. You can't change yesterday, but you can change today and tomorrow. Abraham Lincoln said, "The best way to predict the future is to create it." If you want your child to have a bright future, it's up to you to create one. That usually involves taking actions that displease your children. "What do you mean I have to apologize to my sister?" "I don't want to do my homework." "Do I really have to write a thank-you to Grandma for the sweater?"

You are the parent in your family. Your child is not in control, not even of the electronic devices in your home. If your children are not interacting with the family in a way you consider healthy, it's your responsibility to make a change. If you hold a child accountable, he or she will respond. Parents are to train up children in the way they should go, not the other way around. You need a clear idea of what you want and expect from your children.

Jennifer set up an email account for her eleven-year-old daughter. She knew the password and could see the emails. They were not inappropriate, and she didn't have any problems with her daughter's emails or those her friends were emailing. The problem wasn't the content; it was the new intrusion of email into her daughter's life.

"She wanted to check her emails constantly. She would ask to use the family computer several times after school. How many urgent emails can an eleven-year-old get? She was not as interested in her books or toys after she got that email account."

Jennifer realized she needed to set new limits regarding her daughter's computer use. She communicated the ground rules of how email would work: no checking email until homework and chores were done, a ten-minute daily limit, and no clicking on links unless she (Jennifer) knew they were safe. If her daughter asked to check email more than once, there would be no email that day.

Jennifer cautioned her daughter about spam and communicating with strangers online. She outlined the consequences of what would happen if she broke the rules. Finally she explained that technology works best when it's a tool in your life. It becomes destructive when it becomes the main hub where most of your life is experienced.

We can be a lot like Jennifer's daughter, constantly checking texts and emails to the exclusion of everything else, including our children. You can spend the whole day interfacing with your computer with very little face-to-face contact with the real people you can see. Have you ever seen teenagers sitting in the backseat of a car texting each other instead of talking to each other? This can be true of adults as well. The next generation is at great risk of losing the art of personal conversation. But you can intentionally teach your children to get along and to value others face to face.

Family mealtime is a perfect opportunity to practice the five A+ skills with your children. Ask questions like:

- *Who did you enjoy spending time with at school today? What do you like about him or her?*
- *What is something you are thankful for that happened today?*
- *Did anything happen today to make you feel angry or upset?*
- *When was the last time you apologized to someone or someone apologized to you? What happened?*
- *Which subjects in school are the easiest to pay attention to? The most challenging?*

For more table-talk suggestions, check out www.5LoveLanguages. com, where you'll find questions to get the conversation rolling. Remember to make family meals fun and meaningful. Silence cellphones and turn off the television. As you gather around the table, make it a special time for conversation—not with screens but with each other.

Your home is the training ground for the five A+ skills of affection, appreciation, anger, apology, and attention. The time is now for creating that bright future for your child. The next five chapters are designed to give you practical help in teaching these A+ skills.

"Affection is responsible for nine-tenths of whatever solid and durable happiness there is in our lives."

C. S. LEWIS

chapter three

the A+ skill of
affection

A group of second grade girls and boys were waiting for their Sunday school class to begin. Andrew and Clay played together while a group of girls clustered around art supplies. Another boy entered the room, holding his tablet in the air, taking photos of the class. The boys stopped playing. The girls stopped negotiating for the best markers. Everyone gathered around the boy with the tablet. He started playing a video game, and all eyes were locked on the screen. The once-noisy classroom fell quiet except for the beeping of the video game.

One of the leaders stepped forward. "No electronics in class," she said, reaching for the tablet. "You'll get it back before you go home."

The digital magnet was put away. The children returned to their play and drawing. Voices filled the room once again.

The pull of electronic devices is almost irresistible—for children and adults. With a push of a button, video games and virtual worlds captivate our affection. Without other options, kids can grow more attached to their devices than to real people such as friends, teachers, aunts, or grandpas.

It's ironic that an electronic device that connects us to people around the world can also work simultaneously to separate us from the people at hand. You can have a face-to-face chat with Grandma when she lives in a different state or even a different country; computers can give us that powerful and beautiful connection. But most of the time children are not using their devices to Skype with Grandma. They are watching their favorite cartoon character, playing a new game, or surfing a favorite website. Screen time is quickly replacing face time in the modern home.

Television screens are nothing new to the family landscape. One million homes in the United States had one by 1948.[1] Consider your personal television viewing habits with your children. No doubt your children would feel your affection if you snuggled next to them during their favorite program. But in reality, except for occasional family movie nights, parents and children watch different programs, separately. Parents report that their child's media time provides an opportunity for them to catch up on other things.[2]

Advertisers can sell the romantic notion that a family will bond over watching a movie on a brand-new sixty-inch, flat-screen television. The latest phone will allow you to reach out and see anyone in the world with crystal clarity. But perhaps a more realistic picture is a family who shares an address yet lives separately in their own electronic worlds.

physical presence matters

More than anything, Ben wants to be a good father. He's home every night by 6:00 p.m. After dinner, he sits on the couch with his children, Megan, eight, and Ryan, nine. Ben fiddles with his mobile phone. He checks the news, his stocks, and starts reading an article on the best slopes for skiing in the United States. He's thinking of teaching the kids to ski during Christmas break. Ben is physically present on the couch while the kids watch television. But mentally he's someplace else when focused on his mobile device. That phone is the object of his affection.

Ben's children are observing their dad's absorption with his phone. They want to look busy too. Megan puts in her earbuds and searches for songs on her iPod. Ryan flips through channels. The evening ends, and the scenario replays the next evening.

Our homes are experiencing a subtle shift. Parents and children alike are growing more comfortable with spending increasing amounts of time with devices. Unknowingly we've accepted a trade-off. We're becoming less affectionate toward each other. We might be sharing the same space as our family members but we are not connecting emotionally to each other. Shane Hipps, author of *Flickering Pixels*, writes, "Digital space has the extraordinary ability to create vast superficial social networks, but is ill-suited for generating intimate and meaningful human connection."[3]

When I (Arlene) had a miscarriage at twenty-six weeks, many friends rallied around us. Although a post online saying, "I'm thinking of you," was nice, it did not compare to the comfort of a real hug from a friend who stopped by the house. Physical presence matters. You cannot communicate intimacy through texts, emails, or tweets. The deepest form of affection is given face to face in real time.

As parents, we have a daily golden opportunity to show affection face to face to our children—through a hug, a conversation, clearing the dishes together, or taking a jaunt to the ice-cream shop. Your presence means a great deal to your child, not just your physical presence but your mental and emotional presence. While you are with your child, be all there. Your child will learn from your example. He will see that people who are physically present deserve more affection than digital connections.

making friends

I (Arlene) was on my computer when Noelle, age seven, asked, "Mom, how do you make friends?" Since I was on a social networking site, I assumed she meant online friends. "No, real friends," she replied. I was relieved she wanted to make real friends!

I turned from my computer and looked her in the eye. My mom talk about friendship was forming. "You make friends by being a good friend. You are kind to someone and go out of your way to make her feel special. You ask questions about her life. You are genuinely interested in her."

Noelle asked, "Do you say, 'I want to be your friend'? Maria in school says you have to know someone for two days before you can be friends."

I smiled. "I'm not sure how it works for second graders," I admitted. "Adults don't say, 'I want to be friends,' but we act in a friendly way and then become friends. There's not a rule that says you have to know someone two days to be friends, but it is true that the longer you know someone, the closer you become as friends."

Noelle had another question. "What if I met someone a long time ago, and then I see them again but I can't remember their name. What should I do?"

"Let's role-play," I said. I walked toward Noelle and then stopped. "Oh, I remember you. We met a long time ago. My name is Mommy; what is your name?"

Big brother Ethan chimed in. "I met two kids after school today. Jeff was in fourth grade, and Sean was in sixth. And I initiated!" he said proudly.

Children need guidance when it comes to forming healthy friendships. Home is the ideal place to train children to succeed in their relationships. Take time to answer questions about friendship. My husband, James, has been teaching our kids to initiate conversations and learn names at school (thus Ethan's pride at meeting those two boys). Don't underestimate the role you can play in teaching your child what it means to be a good friend.

The playdates of yesterday were filled with building block castles, making forts, playing store, and dressing up in costumes. The playdates of today are often dominated by screen time. One friend introduces another friend to her favorite television show. Boys play video games together. Instead of talking and imagining together, kids sit next to each other, sharing a handheld device or holding their own devices.

"Yes, there will be another child to play with," Tricia assured her six-year-old daughter, Jane, as they headed for a neighborhood party. When she arrived, Jane spotted two girls who looked about her age. They were on the couch, hunched over a phone, playing a game. Jane said hi and sat down next to one of the girls. They nodded at her and, without a word, continued playing the game. After about five minutes, Jane got up to look for her mom.

"They won't play with me. I want to go home," Jane whispered. Tricia didn't know what to do. She couldn't blame Jane. She had been watching the whole scene and knew that nothing close to real play was happening. "Let's stay for a little while. Maybe some other girls will come," said Tricia.

They stayed another half hour, but no other kids came. The girls eventually stopped playing the video game and switched to watching television. Jane joined them. As they walked back to their house, Jane's mom thought about the party. Jane hadn't gotten to know those girls. They didn't talk or interact. They just sat together while being entertained.

At home, Tricia used the party to talk with Jane about technology. "Wouldn't it have been more fun if you girls played games outside or used that great dollhouse? When you have the chance to play with other girls, it's always best to put away the video games and play instead."

There are plenty of opportunities to use technology, but playdates with friends are special and harder to come by with a family's busy schedule. Don't allow your children to waste that time on screens. Before the playdate, make sure your child and the guest understand: there will be no screen time. After all, becoming good friends happens best face to face.

please like me

Many people derive their self-worth from affirmation from other people. Kids are no different. Everybody wants to be liked. Children in elementary school are now being introduced to social media. In addition to being liked on the playground, now children are wondering how many people "liked" the photo they just posted or how many "friends" they have online.

In an effort to be technologically savvy, teachers in elementary school are showing their students how to engage with blogs inside the classroom. Kids as young as first grade are encouraged to leave comments and digitally engage. They are learning about getting and receiving feedback from other people. Unfortunately, social media can teach kids that the road to popularity is paved by likes and the number of comments and online friends one has.

It's hard enough for an adult to deal with disparaging comments online or a lack of comments, which communicates, "No one is interested in me." Imagine how much harder it is for children who don't yet possess the emotional maturity to cope with the digital world. Researchers have proposed a new phenomenon called "Facebook depression," defined as depression that develops when preteens and teens spend a great deal of time on social media sites, such as Facebook, and then begin to exhibit classic symptoms of depression.[4]

As your child grows into a teenager, he needs the firm foundation of being liked for who he is by real people he knows. Online "likes" are often based on performance, appearance, or shock value. This affection is conditional. Your child needs to experience the unconditional love that comes from God and from you. Only unconditional love can prevent problems such as resentment, feelings of being unliked, guilt, fear, and insecurity. That kind of love is not found online.

Every child is asking the question, "Do you like me?" By limiting her social media, you will help your child find the answer in real people who can shower her with affection instead of an online community that can be fickle and cruel.

desensitized

When my (Arlene's) daughter Lucy was three, she jumped in front of me, waved a pretend light saber, and proclaimed, "I'm going to kill you!" Her eyes were sparkling, and she was laughing. She was playing, but those words were certainly ill-fitted for her mouth. I wondered where she got that expression. She was probably imitating Ethan doing battle with his Star Wars mini figures. We don't watch Star Wars movies or television shows because of our kids' ages, yet here was little Lucy saying, "I'm going to kill you!"

I did not scold Lucy; she didn't know better. Neither did I let it slide. I told her it wasn't right to say, "I'm going to kill you" and that instead she should try, "I'm going to get you!" or "Watch out, here I come!" She hasn't used the word *kill* since that encounter. When we correct our children about their language, teaching them which words are appropriate and which aren't, they listen.

Our children are profoundly influenced by what they watch. They pick up words, phrases, and values from television shows, YouTube videos, and virtual worlds. If we leave our children unattended with their screens, we must be prepared to accept the consequences. They may be using language that's coarse or too mature. They may be developing a stronger affection for their devices than for people. After all, devices bend to your every whim and people don't.

Researchers are concerned that when screen time goes up, empathy goes down. Kids are exposed to violence in video games, which can desensitize them to pain in others, bullying, and acts of violence. The ease of online friendships—you can just move on to another friend if someone is bugging you—can make real-life relationships too frustrating. A University of Michigan study found that college students don't have as much empathy as they used to. College students are about 40 percent lower in empathy than they were twenty or thirty years ago.[5]

You want to teach your child to value others. However, the digital world tends to make a child more me-centered than other-centered. The technological world consists of games, tweets, posts, and virtual worlds designed to make your child feel like the center of the universe.

Jason is a twenty-two-year-old who grew up playing video games. But when he was a teenager, he wasn't playing the massively multiplayer on-line games that are popular today. In these highly addicting games, large numbers of players from anywhere in the world compete at once. His fourteen-year-old brother, Danny, plays for several hours a day.

"My brother used to be kind and polite when he was younger. But now he's much different," said Jason. "After months of constant gaming, he has become rude and difficult to be around. He swears a lot more since he got his own console in his room. I think playing violent games with a bunch of strangers has a lot to do with why he acts like that."

Kids are not only at risk of becoming desensitized to violence, they are bombarded with sexual content from an early age. More than 75 percent of prime-time television programs contain sexual content, yet for only 14 percent of sexual incidents are any risks or consequences suggested.[6] Not surprisingly, youth exposure to sexual content on television can be used to predict adolescent pregnancy.[7] Mobile phones have enabled kids to view sexual information and pornography anywhere. In one study, 20 percent of teenagers admitted sexting (sending sexual text messages and/or explicit images).[8] Preteens send or post nude pictures of them-selves because they've been dared to or because they want attention. It's easier than ever to look for love in all the wrong places. Parents must guard what their children see with great care.

still the window to the soul

When you look at a person's eyes, there's a sense that you are looking into his soul. Sight is a precious gift. Those who are blind but once had sight can tell you what an invaluable gift it is. The next time you are with your child, try looking at your child's arm or foot while you're talking to him.

Then fix your attention on his face and look into the eyes. See the difference? You can use this exercise to illustrate the value of eye contact to your child. (For more drills to help your child role-play, look for "Drills for Grown-Up Social Success" at www.5LoveLanguages.com).

Jocelyn Green, coauthor of *The 5 Love Languages Military Edition*, has two young children. She says,

> One thing I have noticed with youth is the lack of eye contact. Even when I buy something at the drug store, the checkout clerk can do the entire transaction without ever looking at me. I believe it's symptomatic of our screen-oriented relationships. That's why my husband and I are very deliberate in coaching our children to look people in the eyes, observe body language, and respond to questions when asked.[9]

Making eye contact used to be considered a common courtesy. Now it will set your children apart from others if they learn this basic skill. There is something that happens between two people when they look in each other's eyes. Parents and children who look in each other's eyes experience the deepest kind of communication. We can talk across the room or across the hall. We can talk loudly from one room into another. But you form a much deeper connection when you are face to face, eyes looking at one another. Eye contact adds visual and emotional contact.

We talk about people gazing into each other's eyes for hours when they are falling in love. Husbands and wives should continue to look into each other's eyes long after the wedding ceremony. The same is true for children and parents. It's healthy for children to watch their parents making eye contact with each other, hugging, kissing, and holding hands. It brings security to a child when his parents are affectionate with one another.

There are some things you can communicate with a child effectively by texting or talking on the phone. Things like "I'm parked by the main entrance" and "I'm on my way" can be timely and helpful. But the bulk of parenting requires direct eye contact. You can't look a child in the eye through a text. You can't hug a child through the cellphone. You can't instruct a child in a 140-character tweet. The eyes are the window to your child's soul. Look into them often, and don't be in a rush to get to the next thing on your agenda. Just lingering for a few seconds of eye contact can make a big difference in the level of affection your child feels from you.

tell me a story

Diane was planning a Christmas party for her teenage daughter and her friends. She decided to also invite a group of seventy-year-old grandmothers from her church. As Diane made the finishing touches on the meal in the kitchen, she encouraged the older women to share what was the first gift they remembered receiving at Christmas. Before long, teenaged girls were tucked under the arms of the older women, entranced by charming stories of long ago. They all laughed and cried together, becoming fast friends.

When the party was coming to a close, the teens told Diane that their favorite part of the party wasn't the meal, games, or gifts. Their favorite part had been listening to the stories. When you share your stories, there's a close bond created that technology cannot beat. Stories weave families together. *Why does Grandpa have that medal in his room? How did you and Mommy meet? When you went to camp for the first time, were you scared?* These conversations are family glue!

My (Arlene's) husband, James, can tell story after story of his childhood. He has a great memory—and he was a naughty boy so he has plenty of juicy tales. Time and time again our kids will plead, "Please, Daddy, tell us another story from when you were a kid." When he was in second grade, his family was vacationing in Toronto, Canada. They entered a huge colorful marketplace, bustling with people. James is the youngest of four kids. He quickly got distracted and let go of his mother's hand. He stared at the grand display of toys, and when he looked around, his family was nowhere in sight. He was lost in a big city. After walking around for a long time, he finally decided to look for the car. He searched for his license plate that read "New York," found the right car, and sat down. Three hours later, his poor family arrived at the car. That was the last time James ever got lost. His mom told him, "The rules have changed. From now on, you are to hold my hand. It's your job to follow me."

What stories can you share with your kids over a meal today? You can tell them about your first job, best friend in elementary school, or favorite movie when you were growing up. Sharing stories deepens your family relationships. Don't allow technology to steal time from family storytelling. Those stories will root your children in your affection.

filling the love tank

Every child has an emotional tank, a place of emotional strength that can fuel him through the challenging days of childhood and adolescence. Just as cars are powered by reserves in the gas tank, our children are fueled from their emotional tanks. As parents, it's our job to fill our children's emotional tanks with the affection they need to grow healthy and strong. Spending two hours playing a video game cannot add fuel to a child's emotional tank.

There are five ways all people speak and understand emotional love. They are physical touch, words of affirmation, quality time, gifts, and acts of service. If you have several children in your family, chances are they speak different languages, for just as children often have different personalities, they may hear in different love languages. You will learn more about the love languages and screen time in chapter 10.

Young children are not subtle about asking for our love. I (Arlene) think my little Lucy's favorite word in the dictionary is *HUGGIE!* Young kids will squirm to get on your lap, make noise, and sometimes act inappropriately just to get your affection. When we realize they are really pleading for us to spend time with them, to hold them, to give ourselves to them in a personal manner, we will remember that we have the precious responsibility to fill their love tanks.

Older kids may not be as vocal as young ones, but the need for affection is equally important. Especially against the electronic background of ever-present screens, our kids must feel our love and affection in a real way. Otherwise, the temptation to look for affection in the wrong places becomes too strong. With your guidance, your child can learn to give and receive affection in the way God intended, through healthy human relationships.

"Feeling gratitude isn't born in us—it's something we are taught, and in turn, we teach our children."

—JOYCE BROTHERS

chapter four

the A+ skill of
appreciation

Jesse waits with a bunch of rowdy third graders in the lunch line. The cafeteria lady puts milk, chicken nuggets, apple slices, and a cookie on his tray. He takes his tray and walks toward a long table, without a word of thanks or even making eye contact with the cafeteria lady.

It's Christmas Day, and Sarah can't wait to open her gift. She tears the paper off the small box. "We hope you like it," Sarah's mom says with a big smile. The box opens to reveal a shiny new, yellow iPod shuffle.

"Oh no!" Sarah sighs with disappointment. "I wanted the turquoise one!"

Gabrielle stands over the kitchen sink, washing a pile of dishes from dinner. Her feet are aching from working retail all day. The kids don't offer to help; they didn't even bother to clear the table. Come to think of it, no one said thank you for dinner either.

There are two little words in the English language that can soften any heart, deeply connect, and give hope to the weary. You probably know these two words, but perhaps you haven't heard them used much in your home lately. They are *thank you.*

Imagine the difference it would make in the cafeteria lady's world if Jesse and the other children would look her in the eyes and say thank you. Imagine if Sarah on Christmas Day would say, "Oh, thank you! I love it!" and then ask her parents later if she might exchange it for a different color. Imagine if Gabrielle's kids pitched in with the dishes and thanked her for the meal.

A heart of gratitude can turn a bad day into a good one and an unhappy child into a happy one. But gratitude doesn't come naturally to children— or adults, for that matter. Your child must be taught to say thank you.

the enemy of gratitude: indulgence

Don's son Maxwell, age five, was obsessed with the train set he had seen in the store window. Whenever they went to the mall, Maxwell would pull his parents to the toy shop and beg for the train set. It was expensive, but Maxwell's birthday was coming up. His parents bought the set and wrapped it up for his birthday. They were delighted because they knew how much Maxwell wanted the train.

When Maxwell saw that train, he exploded with joy. He was so happy and thrilled with his new train set. He set it up in the living room and played with it every day for two weeks. After a month went by, the train went unused most days. Now Maxwell had his sights on a helicopter. He talked his parents into buying it for him. Then he begged for a robot, a play guitar, and a scooter. His parents grew weary of his nagging and figured buying these things would make Maxwell happy. But instead of being grateful, he just wanted more and more. It seemed the more toys he had, the more he wanted. "The more we gave him, the less he appreciated it," said Don.

When a child is given unrestrained gratification of his own appetites and desires, he becomes spoiled and selfish. Don't try to make your child happy or rescue him by indulging his whims. You don't need to supply your children with every game and gadget you can afford. The kind of happiness that comes from acquiring things is temporary at best. We do children a great disservice when we give them everything they want. This is not how the real world works.

Many times children will say, "But everyone else has one!"—which, incidentally, is never true. Just because a child says he wants something isn't your signal to scramble in order to get it for him. Parents have asked, "What if my child's love language is gifts? Won't she be hurt or feel unloved if I don't get what she wants?" Even if your child's love language is gifts, you still don't have to provide everything she wants. Think of how God parents us. He doesn't give us everything we want. Sometimes He says no to what we want, other times He says wait, and sometimes He says yes. God is our example in parenting. At times, we will say no to our kids because we know what they are asking for is not going to help them. Other times we make them wait because they are not ready for what they desire or it's not in the budget.

Children who make their parents feel guilty or like they are bad parents because they don't give them certain things must be challenged early on. Most of us recognize that the younger generation has a strong entitlement mentality. "I deserve that" and "You owe that to me" are attitudes kids can easily pick up. But the only thing a child is really entitled to is his parents' love. Not to keep up with the Joneses. Not a brand-new bike or iPad. Just love. Every child deserves to be loved by his or her parents. If a child has your unconditional love, he has the greatest asset in the world. If we as parents can realize it's love that our children need most, and not things, we will stop trying to buy our children's happiness with possessions.

We can help our children develop a more sensible range of wants and a deeper appreciation for what they have. Teach your children to wait for what they want. Sometimes they have to wait until they earn enough money or until they are old enough to have a particular toy or device. Ultimately they will enjoy the toy more if they have waited for it and worked hard to earn it.

The most bored children in the world are teenagers whose parents gave them everything they wanted. There comes a time when there's nothing else they can reach for. Many of them start reaching for forbidden fruit. They get bored with the normal things of life and start experimenting with drugs, sex, or other destructive influences, causing great pain to the family.

There's tremendous value in letting children learn that you have to wait for some things in life. Remember you are raising future adults. That may be hard to keep in mind when you're toting around a diaper bag, but it isn't any less true. If your children grow up with everything they want, what kind of adults will they become? You probably know a young couple who, though they can't afford it, buy everything in their first year of marriage, and then, a few years later, declare bankruptcy. They had never learned how to wait for what they wanted or to appreciate what they had.

gratitude through the ages

Nothing in life is more important than knowing how to build positive relationships with people and God. If you equip your child to build positive relationships, it affects their future business, marriage, parenting, emotional and spiritual well-being. Having a thankful heart serves as the foundation. Maybe you've observed your toddler rant and rave, and you wonder how there can be a thankful heart inside that two-foot tyrant. Are young children capable of showing gratitude and, if so, at what age?

There's not an arbitrary age when a switch flips and a child can suddenly comprehend and express gratitude. Yet rather early on, around age two or three, you can begin to teach children the concept of sharing and saying thank you. There are good habits kids can assimilate early—things like saying thank you to a parent at mealtime or after receiving a gift. The sooner you start those expressions of gratitude, the more likely your child is going to connect to incorporating the kinds of courtesies that build relationships.

Grateful kids realize that the whole world doesn't revolve around their wants and needs. Things like freshly washed laundry, a hot meal, and a cleaned up toy room don't just happen automatically. A mom or a dad has to work hard to make those things happen. Realizing that others have gone out of their way to help doesn't come naturally to a child, but they can learn it.

By age two or three, children can talk about being thankful for specific objects, people, pets, and experiences. A toddler can say, "Thank you for the doll" or "That was fun. Thanks!"

By age four, in addition to being thankful for material things like toys, they can express thanks for hugs, affirming words, and other caring acts.

By five or six, kids can write their own thank-you notes with some help from Mom or Dad. They can give a hug to a loved one, look them in the eye, and express thanks. They can call a relative who lives far away to say thank you for a birthday gift.

By seven or eight, children can keep a notebook for writing down a few things they are thankful for each day.

By nine, many children are mature enough to help with a service project with those who are less fortunate. Volunteering in a food bank or convalescent center can serve as a real eye-opener for kids.

By their tween and teen years, your children can do just about anything adults can to show and communicate gratitude to others. They can bake cookies, write thank-you letters to teachers and youth leaders, or participate in a short mission trip. My (Gary's) fourteen-year-old granddaughter recently cooked an entire meal for her family to thank her mom and dad for the work they do every day.

I (Arlene) remember playing a wooden game with pegs in it with my daughter Lucy, who was three. Moving the pegs wherever she wanted, she didn't follow any rules. I didn't mind; the game was too advanced for her age. She decided the game was over and yelled, "Loser! Loser!" pointing at me and grinning with delight. "Lucy, that is rude," I instructed. "You don't point at people and call them losers." We played three more "rounds" and then put away the game. To my delight and surprise, Lucy looked up into my face and said, "Thank you for playing with me for a while. Thank you for playing the game with me."

She may have been off with her "Loser! Loser!" comment but her "Thank-you" at the end made up for that and more. Even at a young age, kids can do far more than we sometimes think they can. You don't have to wait until your children reach a certain age before teaching them about gratitude. All throughout their childhood, you can model a thankful heart and train them to express thanks in age-appropriate ways. These skills will serve them for a lifetime.

10 screen-free ways to cultivate a thankful heart in your child

FAMILY TREE. Have your child draw a family tree, complete with parents, grandparents, siblings, aunts, uncles, and cousins. Discuss positive things you enjoy about each person. Pray and thank God for your family.

Scavenger Hunt. Equipped with paper and pen, go through your room and write down all the items you are thankful to have.

Save Money for a Cause. Sponsor a child through a relief organization, buy a well for a needy family in an emerging country, or send toys to a poor family at Christmas. You can keep a jar in a central location so everyone can contribute loose change and bills. Be creative: maybe skip dessert for a week and put the money you save into the jar.

Play Grateful Hot Potato. Have your family sit in a circle. It doesn't matter if you use a potato, ball, rolled-up socks, or stuffed animal. The object of the game is to say something you are grateful for and then pass the hot potato to the next family member. If you can't come up with anything new to say within five seconds, you are out.

Write a Treasured Note. Have your child think of someone important in her life: a teacher, coach, pastor, or relative. Have her complete this sentence in her note: You have made a difference in my life because _____.

Keep a Gratitude Journal. Have your child write up to five things he or she feels grateful for each day. At the end of the week, have your child read the list aloud to the family.

OPERATION CARE PACKAGE. Have your kids outgrown some clothes or toys? Find someone in your school or church who has a child who would really benefit from those old clothes and toys. Make a big care package and deliver it to that family.

Rice Again? You can teach your children to appreciate the variety of foods they have by offering them only rice for one day. Don't worry, it's not going to hurt your child for one day, and it will be a memorable lesson on how many children of the world eat every day.

Be a Good Neighbor. Bake cookies or brownies for your neighbors just because. Attach a note of appreciation ("Thanks for being a great neighbor!") and have your children sign it. Deliver the cookies together so your children can see how the neighbors respond.

FIGHT HUNGER. Volunteer at a food bank to help stock food in a warehouse, assemble bags of food, or distribute food. Talk about your experience over family dinner.

from *got-to* to *get-to*

I (Arlene) grew up as an only child. My husband, who is the youngest of four, is quick to point out that although I wasn't "spoiled rotten," I was for sure spoiled. The first time I did my own laundry was as a freshman in college. James was doing his own laundry by second grade.

By participating in household chores, children realize that keeping a house takes effort and they become more appreciative. Following in James's footsteps, our kids are doing laundry, emptying the dishwasher, and completing chores around the house. One afternoon I was writing and my kids, then six and eight, were arguing about who would clean the toilets. But they were actually arguing because they both *wanted* to clean the toilets. Apparently watching the water turn blue and swishing the cleaner around with a brush is actually fun.

Use every opportunity to turn the *got-to's* in life into *get-to's*. For most of us, cleaning toilets is a got-to but to my kids in that moment it was a get-to. Consider the different attitudes expressed in these two statements: "I have to go to school" and "I get to go to school."

Harvard lecturer and author Shawn Achor was invited to go on a speaking tour through Africa. One of the stops was a school next to a shantytown where there was no electricity and hardly any running water. He realized that many of his stories about Harvard and privileged American students would not translate. Trying to find a common point of reference, he asked the group of children, "Who here likes to do schoolwork?" He expected the universal distaste of homework to provide a common bond, but instead he found the opposite. Ninety-five percent of the children raised their hands and smiled enthusiastically.[1] Those children saw schoolwork as a privilege—as a *get-to*—something their parents never had the chance to achieve.

We all have something to learn about gratitude from those schoolchildren. They have only a few articles of clothing to call their own, yet they are grateful for what they have. One morning before church, I (Arlene) laid out a new, pink corduroy dress in Noelle's room. "Here's what you are wearing today," I said. She stared at the dress, underwhelmed. "I don't really like that," she finally said. "Well, I bought it for you, and you're wearing it anyway. What don't you like about it?" I asked. "It looks like Cinderella's work dress." I forced her to wear the dress, but she was not happy about it.

Our kids *get to* wear clothes that others would treasure (even if that dress *did* look like Cinderella's work dress). It's our job to teach them the value of what they have. They can be thankful they *get to* wear clean clothes. They *get to* scrub a toilet because they are fortunate enough to have running water, a necessity much of the world does without. They *get to* go to school and receive an excellent education. Many children don't have the opportunity to learn to read.

That small change in attitude and gratitude will make a huge difference in your children's life as they grow into adulthood. Noelle and I were shopping in a department store when she was about eighteen months old. She had a huge smile on her chubby face. The saleslady wore nice clothes, but she also wore a sour disposition. She joked to Noelle, "You're smiling now because you're riding around in that stroller. Just wait until you have a job and have to work all day. We'll see if you're smiling then!"

I thought that even if I sat that lady in a fancy cart and pushed her around all day in the department store, she would find something to complain about. When you view your work as a got-to instead of a get-to, it negatively affects your mood and performance. You can give your children an incredible gift by teaching them to be grateful—at work or at play.

every day is thanksgiving

Giving thanks is the star of Thanksgiving Day, but if that's the only time a family verbalizes what they are thankful for, it isn't enough. Gratitude is something children learn best by watching it modeled in everyday life. A father can say to a mother (or vice versa), "I really appreciate your work in putting this meal together. It's delicious." If children constantly hear parents appreciating one another, they will learn to do the same. Look for things to thank your spouse and children for each day. *Thank you for taking out the trash. I really appreciate you sorting out the mail. Thank you for the hug.* If saying thank you becomes a way of life in your home, your children will move into the world always being grateful for what other people do for them.

When you as a parent realize it's your responsibility to model thanksgiving to your child, it changes the way you see the world. You begin to look for blessings, and it becomes easier to notice the hard work of others. I (Arlene) was at a coffeehouse with my kids. I looked at the barista's name, Marissa. I told my kids loud enough so she could hear, "Did you know that Marissa has to know how to make a hundred different drinks, and that is a challenging job? She is working hard to make Mommy's coffee just right. Thank you, Marissa!" Marissa's face lit up. My kids were learning to appreciate others, and I felt great for making Marissa's day brighter. The giving of thanks blesses everyone involved.

Research shows that grateful people are more resilient and less depressed. Kids who feel and act grateful tend to be less materialistic, get better grades, set higher goals, complain of fewer headaches and stomachaches, and feel more satisfied with their friends.[2] Gratitude is also linked to lower levels of aggression. Kids who express thanks are more empathetic toward others, making them less prone to aggression and violent behaviors.[3]

My (Arlene's) son, Ethan, and I were at Disneyland without the other family members to celebrate his ninth birthday. He got to pick all the rides and shows he wanted. He gave this much thought, outlining again and again to me the particular rides we would enjoy. I'm sure he lay in bed many nights dreaming about his day at Disneyland.

One of the rides he wanted to go on was the monorail, so we planned to ride it at the very end of the day. We arrived at the monorail station five minutes before the park closed, ready for our last hurrah. But it closed one hour before the park closed! We stood motionless in front of that sign. I could see Ethan's countenance fall flat. We had missed it. A gray cloud had descended on the end of our otherwise perfect day. "I'm sorry we missed it, Ethan. I didn't expect for it to close so early."

"I can't believe we missed it," he mumbled.

"Let's make that souvenir penny at the exit," I suggested.

After a few minutes, I started talking about all the wonderful things we had been able to do that day. *Remember how there wasn't a line at Autopia? That was so neat how the chimney sweep from* Mary Poppins *said happy birthday to you from the parade!* With every step toward the exit, Ethan grew more even-keeled and grateful for what had happened instead of upset about what hadn't. By the time we got to the souvenir penny, he seemed back to his happy self. Later in the car, he said those magic words, "Thank you so much, Mom, for taking me to Disneyland today."

You can help your children give thanks even when things don't go according to plan. Let them experience for themselves that good feeling of peace and contentment that comes as a result of learning to say thank you every day.

appreciation goes viral

As your children grow into teenagers, you may find that much of their communication with friends happens over a screen through texts, instant messages, and posts. The A+ skill of appreciation needs to happen online as well as off-line. When our children interact with friends via screens, we want them to use words that are positive and appreciative.

Unfortunately, many screen-savvy teenagers are not taught to treat people with respect and courtesy online. Navigating friendships on a screen can seem more transactional than human. You can delete friends who bother you and just get new ones. People can be treated like a commodity; they are there for your convenience to meet your needs.

Teens can say very hurtful things to each other through texting. Letters that look like gibberish to an adult can carry offensive and hurtful messages to a texting teenager. While our children are younger, we must teach them to value and appreciate others face to face and also whenever they communicate electronically.

A group of high school students in Iowa City are making a positive splash with their screen time. Jeremiah Anthony created a Twitter feed to his fellow West High School classmates in order to fight against the tide of cyber bullying. His mission: to tweet positive comments about his classmates. He and his friends have tweeted more than 3,500 compliments to specific students ranging from "You are the man, one of the best runners West has right now" to "Keep being loving and caring of all." These tweets were featured on national television, an indicator of how unusual it is to find a source of appreciation online.[4]

You can teach your children to go against the tide. When others tear down, they can build up. When others concentrate on accumulating more possessions, they can outdo others with acts of generosity. When others are finding their best friends online, they can find them off-line. When others complain about their lives, they can be grateful.

The power of gratitude can change your child's attitude and actions for the better, both in the real world and the digital world. Training your child to think, speak, and text gratefully begins right at home, with the thankful words and actions you model.

"When angry count to ten before you speak.
If very angry, count to one hundred."

—THOMAS JEFFERSON

chapter five

the A+ skill of
anger management

It's recess and Mrs. Granger's first grade class is outside playing. Catherine and her friend are bouncing the ball back and forth.

"I want the ball," says John as he lunges toward the girls.

"No," says Catherine. "We are playing with it!"

A few minutes later, John is back. He snatches the ball and gives Catherine a hard shove, pushing her to the ground. She begins to cry. Mrs. Granger sees John push Catherine down and rushes to the scene.

"John," she says, looking into his eyes. "We use our hands for clapping." The recess bell rings, and Mrs. Granger helps Catherine go inside. John may have learned that hands are for clapping, but what he really needed to learn was dealing with his anger. Mrs. Granger didn't force John to take responsibility for pushing down a fellow classmate. Instead he was given the vague instruction that hands are for other things, like clapping.

What else could Mrs. Granger have said? It would have been better to say, "John, it was wrong for you to push Catherine down. You may not treat anyone like that on the playground. You will not go out at recess tomorrow for your consequence." Then she could have asked a few questions to help John process what had happened. "John, what made you so angry? How do you think it made Catherine feel when you pushed her? What could you do differently next time?"

No one has to teach children to experience anger; that happens automatically. Our task is to teach them to manage their anger. When your child gets angry, don't try to distract him by offering a video game or his favorite cookie. Distractions, delays, or deflections won't help your child learn to process emotions in a healthy manner.

As I (Gary) talk to parents across the country, most are eager to learn how to help their children in this important area of development. I have shared the following principles with many parents in counseling and in parenting workshops. They are simple to understand but not necessarily easy to do.

watch how I do it

Because of the nature of the parent-child relationship, parents are the most influential persons in developing a child's pattern of anger management. This should encourage us because it gives us an opportunity to give our children positive anger management skills. On the other hand, this can be a frightening reality if we are prone to loud tirades or icy silence.

Fortunately, adults can learn to change destructive patterns and establish new, healthier models of processing anger. Scott and Dee came into my office because their son Matt, age fourteen, had a terrible problem with anger, yelling and screaming at his parents constantly.

"I don't think he should be allowed to talk to us that way," said Dee. "I scream at Matt, and when he leaves, I scream at Scott. I tell him he shouldn't let Matt talk to us that way. I'm a wreck. Maybe I'm the one who needs help."

Dee grew up in an Italian home where everybody screamed at everybody, but when it was over, it was over. Scott on the other hand, grew up with a father who yelled and lost his temper once in a while. When he got loud, Scott got silent. Dee's response to anger was to yell. Scott's basic response to anger was to be silent. They learned certain responses from their parents, and now they were modeling poor anger management to their son.

Often adults do not consciously think of their own anger management until they observe their children's response to anger. Many times children mirror what they have learned from parents. Since Matt was a child, when Dee was upset by his behavior, she had expressed her anger by screaming and yelling. Matt now expresses his anger in a similar way.

Through several sessions I worked with Dee and Scott, helping them share their anger with each other in an open, loving, noncondemning manner. Later Dee and Scott told Matt they realized their model of handling anger was not very positive and that they were going to counseling. Matt seemed pleased, although he didn't say much at the time. However, they knew he was getting the message when one night as Dee was getting a bit tense, Matt said, "Mom, I think you need to get the three-by-five card and read it to Dad."

Dee said, "I think you're right, Matt. Thanks."

They were really shocked one night about two months later when Matt walked into the room holding the three-by-five card and read, "I'm feeling angry right now, but don't worry—I'm not going to attack you. But I do need your help. Is this a good time to talk?" They both broke into laughter. Matt said, "No guys, I'm really serious. I'm angry, and I need to talk with you about it." They gave Matt their undivided attention. Matt was mirroring the transformation he had seen in his parents. Dee and Scott were learning to deal with anger constructively—and so was their son. When we parents learn to handle our own anger in a healthier manner, we will be in the position to guide our children in processing their anger.

desperately seeking parental guidance

Just as a child must be taught to tie her shoes or ride a bicycle, so a child must be taught how to handle anger. A child has only two ways to express anger: verbally and behaviorally. Each of these can be positive or negative. Behaviorally, a child may express anger by pushing, shoving, striking, throwing objects, pulling hair, or beating his own head against the wall. Obviously, these are negative responses to anger. On the other hand, leaving the room, counting to one hundred aloud, or taking a walk outside are mature behavioral responses to anger that allow the child to cool down and process anger in a constructive manner.

On the verbal side, the child may yell and scream condemning statements or may use profanity or name-calling—all destructive ways of verbalizing anger. But the mature child may acknowledge that he is angry and ask for an opportunity to discuss his complete concerns. Your task as a parent is to take your child where he is and help him move toward more constructive ways of processing anger.

If your child is screaming at you in anger, listen! Calmly ask questions and let the anger be expressed. The more questions you ask and the more intently you listen, the more likely his volume will decrease. Concentrate on the reason your child is angry, not on the way he is expressing it. If he thinks he was wronged, the anger will not go away until he feels you have heard and understood the complaint.

You may be asking, "Should I let my child yell at me?" Obviously yelling is not an appropriate way to handle anger. However, at the moment, you want to hear the child's concerns. Later you can talk about a healthier way to share concerns. Some of us expect our teenagers to be more mature than we are. I remember the teen who said in my office, "My dad yells and screams at me while telling me to stop yelling and screaming at him." When parents say, "You are not going to talk to me like that. Now shut up and go to your room," they are driving the child's anger underground.

If parents do not hear the child's complaints and seek to understand why the child feels that way, the child's anger will be internalized and later show up in the child's behavior. Psychologists call this passive-aggressive behavior. The child is passive on the outside, but inside the anger is growing and will eventually express itself in aggressive behavior, such as low grades, drug experimentation, sexual activity, "forgetting" to do homework, or some other behavior the child knows will upset the parent. If parents understood the extreme danger of passive-aggressive behavior, they would make every effort to listen to their children when they are angry, to hear the issues carefully, to seek to understand, and to find a resolution.

This doesn't mean that the parent must always do what the child is requesting. The child's anger is often distorted—that is, rooted in a perceived wrong rather than a definitive wrong. It's triggered by a disappointment, an unfulfilled desire, a frustrated effort, or a bad mood—none of which have to do with any genuine wrongdoing. You can help your child ask two questions to determine the validity of anger: "What wrong was committed?" and "Am I sure I have all the facts?"

When your child is angry, you can give him the commonsense advice to count to ten (or one hundred for older kids) until his anger cools down. Then you ask him to complete the sentence, "I am angry because _____." Seven-year-old Thomas was upset because his younger sister, Kayla, wrote all over his homework. That was the wrong committed. Next you would gather facts. Did she do it on purpose, or was it an accident? The smirk on her face, followed by a confession, tells you Kayla did it on purpose. Kayla apologized to Thomas, and her markers were taken away for a few days.

Each anger experience gives the parent an opportunity to guide the child through the anger episode, deal with the issues, and find a resolution. Each time this is done, the child becomes a bit more mature in verbalizing his anger. Unfortunately, with increased screen time for both kids and parents, many of these teaching opportunities pass by because family members are too busy and distracted to deal with the root of their anger flare-ups. Parental guidance is desperately needed to help children handle anger responsibly.

"good" versus "bad" anger

"GOOD" ANGER (Definitive)	"BAD" ANGER (Distorted)
Definition: Anger toward any kind of genuine wrongdoing, mistreatment, injustice, or breaking of laws.	**Definition:** Anger toward a perceived wrongdoing where no wrong occurred.
Sparked by: Violation of laws or moral code.	**Sparked by:** People who hurt or irritate us, stress, fatigue, unrealistic expectations.
How to recognize: If you can answer yes to the questions, "Was a wrong committed?" and "Do I have all the facts?"	**How to recognize:** Feelings of frustration or disappointment feed the anger.
What to do: Either confront the person or decide to overlook the offense.	**What to do:** Halt the anger, and gather information to process your anger.

initiating conversations about anger

My (Arlene's) children love to act out different scenarios, so why not practice being angry through drama? It's easier to teach principles to your children about anger when they are *not* angry. In the heat of the moment, no child is particularly open to a lecture.

I gave my two daughters, ages four and seven, the following scenario: Noelle walks in the room to discover her younger sister, Lucy, wearing Noelle's favorite dress, complete with shoes and tiara.

72

Scene One:

Noelle (yelling): Lucy! You can't wear my things! Take off that dress. Give me back my shoes and tiara! (Noelle pulls the shoes off Lucy's feet and grabs the tiara.)

Scene Two:

Noelle (calmly): Lucy, you look very beautiful. But there is something wrong. You didn't ask to borrow my things. Please take them off, or else I am going to get Mom.

Believe me, scene one was much more realistic! Acting out these scenarios was not only fun, but it also helped us move into a brief talk about anger and how to express it responsibly.

There are many ways and places for parents to give verbal instruction to children about matters related to anger. Depending on the age of the child, the following are effective ways of helping a child understand and process anger effectively.

For the young child, *reading and discussing Bible stories* that focus on anger provide an interesting format for instruction. Such stories as Cain and Abel, Joseph and his eleven brothers, Jonah and his anger toward God, and Jesus and His anger toward the money changers all provide key insights into understanding anger.

Memorizing key Scriptures is also an excellent method of instruction for children. Consider these verses:

- Fools give full vent to their rage, but the wise bring calm in the end. Proverbs 29:11
- Whoever is patient has great understanding, but one who is quick-tempered displays folly. Proverbs 14:29
- "In your anger do not sin": Do not let the sun go down while you are still angry, and do not give the devil a foothold. Ephesians 4:26–27

For older children, *reading and discussing this chapter* could be an excellent way to give instruction about processing anger. Encouraging a child to write a paper on the topic of anger is another method. Your child could interview parents and grandparents for ideas on the source of anger and how to process anger constructively. This could be an enlightening project for an older child or teenager.

Open conversation, allowing your child to ask questions and make comments, could be a springboard not only for discussing anger as a topic, but also to talk about how you have processed anger in the past and what positive changes might be made. In such a family conversation, parents might share with a child their own struggles with anger. This vulnerability creates an atmosphere for a child to express his own struggles or ask questions.

Such conversations can easily be initiated by sharing with the child something you read recently. For example, "I was reading an article the other day on anger. It said that many parents are not aware of how many times they lose their temper with their children and say things that actually hurt the children; the parent never remembers what he said. I was wondering if that could possibly be true of me."

"Well, Mom, since you brought it up . . ."

When you make your anger the focus of the conversation rather than the child's anger, you make it easier for the child to be responsive and reveal his perceptions of the way you handle anger. Such conversations can be extremely instructive to a child—and to the parent.

Your child's need for love is the foundation of meaningful conversation. If your child does not feel loved by you, not only will your child experience greater anger but all your efforts to teach your child are likely to be rejected. You will learn more about the five love languages in chapter 10. Children who feel the security of parental love are much more likely to make wise choices; and when they do make poor choices, they are far more likely to learn from their mistakes and correct future behavior.

Nothing is more fundamental in teaching a child to handle anger than giving the child unconditional love.

do video games fuel anger?

Tony was a typical fifth grader. He liked sports more than schoolwork but did fine in his class. After soccer practice and homework, he was allowed to play video games. He learned about the video games the sixth graders were playing; before long, he was playing them too. Even though the rating of the game was for seventeen-year-olds, all his classmates were playing so his parents figured it was all right.

But after a few months, his parents noticed a change in Tony. His teacher called because he was fighting with another boy in the class and being disrespectful to her. At home, he had little patience for his little sister and would lash out often. If his parents asked what was wrong, it would make him angrier.

When children spend too much time playing video games (especially if they are playing violent games), they will often become grumpy, easily angered, impatient, and argumentative.

Just like adults, children need to rest and recharge. That happens best in outdoor play, settling down with a good book, or hugging and talking to a parent. Relaxation doesn't occur while holding a screen, yet that is how so many children spend all their free time. Without downtime and visual relaxation, children are restless and prone to anger. In addition, screen worlds emphasize speed, so a child raised on computers has little patience for the pace of real life. As a result, when that child has to wait for something, his impatience can quickly morph into frustration and anger.

Many people would like to think that violence in video games, movies, and television do not affect children. The reality is that your child is affected by everything he interfaces with. Screen violence is especially dangerous because it does not teach a child to properly relate to people. First-person shooter video games and television dramas teach a child how to blow up someone, how to destroy someone. You may think, "Well, it's just a game" or "It's on television; it's not real life." But research shows that children who spend a great deal of time watching violent movies and video games are far more likely to be involved in violence themselves. More than a thousand scientific studies and reviews show that significant exposure to media violence increases the risk of aggressive behavior, desensitizes them to violence, and makes them believe the world is a meaner, scarier place than it is.[1]

Video games are especially dangerous because a child is not passively watching a violent act: he is participating in it. The more a child is involved, the more he will get out of the experience. Games also create a system of reinforcement. A child is rewarded for destructive behaviors again and again. If your child plays a violent game or two, it may have little effect. But if he plays a few games several days a week for a period of years, he will not emerge unaffected. There is a correlation between anger and on-screen violence. We need to give extreme guidance regarding what our children are allowed to watch. If you realize your child is playing video games that are not healthy, cut back on that video-game time and make it a goal to eliminate violent video games altogether. Replace those video games with more creative ones that do not involve violence and seek out friends who like to do things besides gaming.

anger online

Your child may be angry not because of the amount of time he is spending with a screen but with the amount of time you are. Many children are frustrated, sad, and angry that they have to compete with screens for their parents' attention. Places that traditionally were spaces for a parent to connect with a child have become phone zones for many adults. A mother uses her phone with a headset in the car, during the park date, and at birthday parties. It's socially acceptable behavior, but what does it communicate to your child? If a child constantly hears, "Hold on a minute dear, I'm on the phone," it communicates that spending time with your child is not as important as what is happening on the phone.

Living in a digital age presents new challenges of how we navigate online relationships and how we pass those habits to our children. One of the problems with technology for kids is that the screen allows an anonymity that can cushion the user from suffering any consequences. Children may not say hateful, angry words to other children to their faces, but they can log on to their computers using a pseudonym and leave angry posts or send nasty emails. Kids can take their anger and frustration out on one another. It's easier than ever to hurt another person—just hit the Send button.

Cyberbullying is deliberately using digital media to communicate false, embarrassing, or hostile information about another person. Kids may send an email to make fun of someone or make that person angry. They may belittle someone in a chat room or post an embarrassing photo on a social networking site. Cyberbullying is a dangerous and lethal pastime for many kids and teenagers.

Nearly 30 percent of adolescents in the United States report some experience with bullying, whether as the victim, the bully, or both.[2] Boys are more likely to engage in physical aggression while girls are more likely to engage in verbal aggression, so you are wise to pay particular attention to how your girl uses screens to communicate. If you discover your child is bullying another child online, one consequence may be to take the phone or iPad away for two days for the first offense. If it happens again, you can restrict her electronic use for a longer period. Once children realize they cannot engage in that kind of online behavior, they will learn to abide by your rules.

You can begin teaching your child online courtesies way before the teenage years. When your child is old enough to send a text or email, it's time to teach them what is and what is not appropriate to say online. You can communicate information: *We'll be at the main gate tomorrow looking for you. I got to eat pizza for dinner tonight.* You can give compliments and encouragement: *Thank you for listening to my story today. I really liked your shirt.* But what you cannot do is use electronics to express anger. Don't ever say anything online about anyone that you would not say if they were sitting in front of you. It will become a harmful habit difficult to break in adulthood if your child learns to use social media to spew insults to get revenge on someone who has made him angry. The ugly words on screens can be read over and over again, making an emotional mark on a child. Teach your children to deal with their anger in real life, not on screens.

Helpful Dialogues for You and Your Angry Child

If your pattern has been to argue with your child, perhaps you can break the pattern by saying,

"I've been thinking about us, and I have realized I am not a very good listener. Usually when you are feeling strongly about something, I also end up getting mad. I really want to be a better listener. In the future, I am going to try to ask more questions and really seek to understand your feelings. I really do think your ideas and feelings are important."

If your child is pushing, yelling, or throwing things, focus on the anger first and the behavior second.

"It's obvious you are very angry. I would like to hear what's bothering you, but we can't talk while you are _____. Want to take a walk and talk about it?"

If you lose your temper with your child, be willing to confess your failures.

"Son, I'm sorry I lost my temper this afternoon. I didn't handle my anger well, and the way I talked to you was not kind. Some of the things I said are not really the way I feel. That was wrong, and I have asked God to forgive me. I want to ask you to forgive me."

Your apology will make it easier for your child to apologize in the future.

"Never ruin an apology with an excuse."

—BENJAMIN FRANKLIN

chapter six

the A+ skill of
apology[1]

It had been a tough day in sixth grade for Alexa. Her best friend, Lindsay, who usually ate lunch with her, picked a different table in the cafeteria with three other girls. At the end of lunch, the girls walked up to Alexa and said mockingly, "Nice shirt." Lindsay just stood there and said nothing. Not only did Alexa feel embarrassed, she didn't understand what Lindsay was doing hanging out with those mean girls.

In between classes, Alexa and Lindsay walked past each other in silence. No eye contact. No conversation. Things went on like this for a few days. A week later, Alexa's phone beeped. It was a text message from Lindsay: "Sorry 4 being mean to u."

Although Alexa was relieved to get the text, she wondered why Lindsay had acted so weird. She felt hurt and betrayed. But she texted back "It's OK," even though it really wasn't.

online apologies fall short

For the sake of efficiency, convenience, and saving face, we can use our electronic devices to do the work of apologizing for us. In trivial matters, an online apology or text message may work fine for things like "Sorry I 4got to feed cat. Can u do it when u get home?" But when you have offended someone or hurt someone's feelings, like the case with Lindsay and Alexa, a text is not enough.

We need to teach children how to apologize in the real world. One of the best ways of doing that is by modeling what a proper apology looks like. If a child hears her father apologizing to her mother because he raised his voice at her, and then she hears Mom forgive him and they hug, that's a powerful lesson. When that same child gets in a loud fight with her brother, she can remember the example of her parents. She will learn to apologize face to face with her family first and then with others outside of the home. Real-life, real-time apologies are extremely important for a child to learn.

Unfortunately, many teens are communicating personal messages such as apologies via text or instant messaging. A child can avoid putting herself in a hard and awkward situation with an electronic *sorry*. Yet those truncated messages shortchange children emotionally. They grow up unable to conduct difficult conversations with the people they truly care about. Hiding from stressful situations negatively impacts their ability to interact with people, now and in the future.

Five lessons about apologizing will benefit your child greatly in life. These keys will open doors to better friendships and closer family relationships. Explain to your child that many kids don't have these keys, but that you would like to give these keys to your child.

key #1: accept responsibility

Teaching your child how to apologize begins with accepting responsibility for wrongdoing. The natural tendency is to blame someone else ("It's his fault!") or an object ("It broke!"). Yet children can learn to accept responsibility even at a young age. Our (Arlene's) family has a minivan, and it is Lucy's job to push the button to close the side door because she's the last one out of the car. We parked near the grocery store, and Lucy, age three, left the van. The door was left wide-open. I was about to mention it when her little voice said, "Oh, I'm sorry. I forgot to close the door." I was not only surprised that she remembered, but I was also surprised that she apologized. She didn't blame a sibling or make an excuse. She took responsibility for her actions. "Good job, Lucy," I said, giving her a big hug. "You are taking responsibility for the door and your own actions. Thank you!"

It is foundational to teach children to take responsibility for their actions and to praise them when they do. A five-year-old can grab a cookie, break it, and then say, "It broke." *It* didn't break; the child broke the cookie. A parent can use that moment to teach this principle of accepting responsibility. "Honey, let's say it a different way: 'I broke the cookie.' The cookie didn't break itself, right? You did it. There's nothing wrong with breaking the cookie. You just have to take responsibility for your own actions and not blame the cookie."

One way to help children learn to accept responsibility for their not-so-noble deeds is to help them rephrase their statements, beginning the sentence with "I." Next, we need to show them that their actions matter to others.

key #2: your actions affect others

The Golden Rule says to treat others the way you would like them to treat you. Every child needs to learn the Golden Rule because it sets the standard for learning how to treat others. It also communicates to the child's mind that some things are good and some are bad, and he or she should aspire to do what is good.

The child begins to think, "If I help my mother set the table, my mother feels happy. If I throw the football inside the house and break the lamp, my mother feels sad. If I say to my father, 'I love you,' my father feels loved. If I say to him, 'I hate you,' my father feels hurt. My words and actions either help people or hurt people. When I help people, I feel good. When I hurt people, I feel bad."

Life affords many opportunities to teach children that our actions affect others. Hillary is six years old and in the first grade. Her brother, Daniel, is four and attends preschool. One afternoon before dinner, they were playing together when her mother heard Hillary say to Daniel, "You are a barbarian. Get out of my room." Daniel burst into tears and ran to his mom. "Hillary called me a barbarian."

His mother gave him a big hug and said, "I know. I will talk to her about that. Why don't you sit here and color in your book while I talk with Hillary?" Her mother walked to Hillary's room and said, "Honey, where did you hear the word *barbarian*?"

"At school. It means a person who does something bad, and Daniel did something bad. He messed up my dollhouse," she said.

"You're right. Daniel needs to say, 'I'm sorry.' But it wasn't very nice to call him a barbarian either. He was hurt that you called him a bad name. So I think you need to say, 'I'm sorry' also."

The mom walked into the kitchen and took Daniel by the hand. "Both of you know that what you did was wrong. Daniel, when Hillary is playing with her dollhouse, it's wrong for you to come in and mess it up. It made her feel upset because she had worked hard to arrange her dollhouse. Hillary, when you called Daniel a barbarian, it upset him very much. You heard him cry and cry because his feelings were hurt. When we hurt someone, we need to say, 'I'm sorry.'"

Hillary paused and then said, "I'm sorry I called you a barbarian."

"Now it's your turn, Daniel," his mother said.

"I'm sorry," he said.

"Sorry for what?" his mother prodded.

"I'm sorry I messed up your dollhouse," he said.

"Good. Now give each other a hug," Mom suggested. They hugged, and then Mom said, "Good. Now Daniel, you go finish coloring, and Hillary, you play in your room. I'll call you both when dinner is ready."

This mother had brought peace to her home by clearly teaching her children that our actions affect other people. And when we do wrong, we need to say, "I'm sorry."

key #3: there are always rules in life

A third key in teaching children to apologize is helping them understand there are always rules in life. We've talked about the Golden Rule, which is most important, but there are other rules designed to help us have a good life. "We don't throw the football inside the house" is a rule most parents have made for obvious reasons. But there are others: We don't take something that doesn't belong to us. We don't tell things that are untrue about others. We don't cross the street without looking both ways. We thank someone who gives us something or says something nice about us.

When parents set rules, the overarching questions should be "Is this rule good for my child? Will it have some positive effect on the child's life?" Here are some practical questions to ask as you decide about a particular rule:

- Does this rule keep the child from danger or destruction?
- Does this rule teach some positive character trait: honesty, hard work, kindness, sharing, and more?
- Does this rule protect property?
- Does this rule teach the child responsibility?
- Does this rule teach good manners?

Once parents have agreed on a rule, the entire family needs to be made aware of it. Unspoken rules are unfair rules. A child cannot be expected to live up to a standard of which he is unaware. Parents carry the responsibility for making sure children understand what the rules are. However, if you come to see that a particular rule is detrimental rather than helpful, then you should be willing to change that rule.

With the rules come consequences when the rules are broken. Consequences should be as closely associated with the rule as possible. For instance, if your child throws the football in the house, he loses the football for two days. It's ideal if the consequences for breaking family rules can be determined and discussed with the family when the rule is made. This gives the child the advantage of knowing ahead of time what the consequences will be, and advance planning often results in more reasonable consequences.

Parents are responsible for making sure the child receives the due consequences if an offense occurs. When parents are permissive one day and let misbehavior slide and the next day come down hard on the child for the same misbehavior, the parents are on the sure road of rearing a disobedient, disrespectful child. Inconsistent discipline is the most common pitfall of parents trying to raise responsible children.

Few things are more important in teaching a child to apologize than establishing clear, meaningful rules and consequences for when the rules are broken, and fairly and firmly administering the consequences when necessary. This process establishes in the mind of the child that "I am responsible for my words and my actions; when I follow the rules, I reap the benefits, and when I choose to break the rules, I suffer the consequences." It develops a sense of morality. Some things are right, and some things are wrong. When I do right, there are good results. When I do wrong, there are negative results. It is this sense of morality that helps the child understand the need for an apology.

key #4: apologies will restore friendships

The fourth key in helping children learn to apologize is helping them understand that apologies are necessary in order to maintain good relationships. When I hurt other people by my words or my behavior, I have established a barrier between that person and me. My hurtful words or actions push people away from me, and without apology, they continue to walk away. The child, teenager, or adult who does not learn this reality will eventually end up alone.

With the help of his mother, Steven is learning this principle. He walked into the house one afternoon, flipped on the TV, and stretched out on the floor. "Why did you come in so early?" his mother, Sharon, asked. "You guys just started playing in the backyard."

"The other boys went home," he answered. "They didn't want to play the new game. I'm tired of playing the same old games. I told them that if they didn't want to play the new game, they could just go home."

The next afternoon when Sharon arrived home from work, she noticed that the neighborhood boys were not playing in the yard. Steven was again stretched out on the floor in front of the TV. "Are you guys not going to play this afternoon?" she asked.

"The guys didn't show up," Steven said. "I think they are playing at the park. I didn't want to go down there."

Over dinner, Sharon asked if Steven had seen any of the guys at school.

"I saw Austin down the hall," he said, "but he didn't see me."

"So none of the guys talked with you today, and none of them came over this afternoon?"

"Nope," he answered.

"Steven, I know you feel bad about this because I know how much you enjoy playing. I appreciate the fact that you like to try new games, but what you said to the guys was pretty harsh."

"I didn't think they would really leave," Steven said. "I didn't even realize what I had said until they all walked away. I'm afraid now they're never going to come back, and I don't have anybody to play with." Tears were forming in Steven's eyes.

Sharon's heart was broken. "I'm going to give you a suggestion, and

I know it is going to be hard to do it. I think you need to apologize to Austin and the other guys. Tell them that you are sorry you got angry and told them to go home, that you have felt bad about it ever since, and ask them to forgive you."

"But Mom, they will think I am a wimp," he said.

"What they think is unimportant. What is important is what you know in your heart, and you know you spoke those words in anger. I don't know whether they will forgive you. But I know that unless you apologize, they are not likely to come back. All of us get angry sometimes," she said, "and we sometimes say things we later regret. But if we are willing to apologize, people will usually forgive us."

After dinner, Steven said, "I'm going to walk to the park, Mom, and see if the guys are there."

"Okay," she said. "Take your cellphone. Call me if you need me." Sharon began to pray. She knew Steven was about to do one of the hardest things he had ever done. But she also knew that if he had the courage to apologize, he was well on the way to becoming a man.

After an hour, Steven came in the house, hot and sweaty. "How did it go?" Sharon asked.

"Cool. The guys were really cool. They said we all get mad sometimes and that it was okay. They asked me to play with them, and we had a good time. I told them we could play in our yard tomorrow."

"Great," his mother said. "Steven, I'm so proud of you. Those guys are fortunate to have a friend like you, and I'm fortunate to have a son like you."

The next afternoon, Sharon came home to find the neighborhood guys playing in the backyard. She breathed a sigh of relief and thanked God that the trouble had been resolved well.

Children must learn that friendships sometimes require honest apologies. The child who learns early that apologies restore friendships has learned one of the major lessons about human relationships.

key #5: the five languages of apology

The final key in teaching children how to apologize is to teach them how to speak the five languages of an apology:

Expressing Regret: "I am sorry."

Accepting Responsibility: "I was wrong."

Making Restitution: "What can I do to make it right?"

Genuinely Repenting: "I'll try not to do that again."

Requesting Forgiveness: "Will you please forgive me?"

The level of proficiency should increase with age—just as, developmentally, children learn to speak a language in a process. Children begin with words they associate with certain objects: *book, shoe, foot.* Then they learn words associated with ideas: *yes, no.* Later they learn to understand sentences: *Let's go. Let's put on the dress.* Then they learn to speak sentences: *I don't like beans. I want to play.* Much later they learn grammatical rules and complex sentence structure. The child's vocabulary and level of comprehension increase year by year. The same is true in teaching children to speak the apology languages.

A two-year-old can learn to say, "I'm sorry," when she pulls the hair of her older sister. Or he could say, "I was wrong. I disobeyed," when he willfully knocks his sippy cup from the table to the floor. Thus, they are learning on the simplest level how to express regret and accept responsibility.

When the three-year-old pushes her brother down and he lies in a puddle of tears, the father may comfort the fallen soldier and teach the three-year-old to say, "I was wrong. I am sorry." And he might even encourage the offender to "go get a Band-Aid for your brother." With running for the Band-Aid, the child is learning to make restitution. Also at a very young age, children can learn to say, "I'll try not to do that again. Will you please forgive me?" and in so doing, they are learning the language of genuinely repenting and requesting forgiveness.

In early childhood (ages two through six), the child can learn to verbalize all five languages of an apology. During these early years, the motivation for apologizing is primarily external—that is, the parents are insisting that the child say "I'm sorry," or "I was wrong," or "I disobeyed." This is done in much the same way as we teach children to say "Thank you," "You're welcome," and "Please." The method is repetition, expectation, and sometimes, the withholding of privileges if the proper word is not spoken. The child learns primarily by outside prompting.

From grade one through grade twelve, the child learns to internalize these concepts and to speak these words from his or her own heart. A child may be able to text a parent or friend, "I was wrong. Please forgive me." That's a good start, but to fully experience that apology and forgiveness, it is best expressed in person. What parent does not take pride when she hears her child say without prompting, "Thank you," "Please," and "You're welcome"? Similarly, the parent knows that her teaching is being effective when she hears a child use one or more of the apology languages without being prompted by the parent.

I (Gary) shall always remember the night my teenage son said to me, "I'm sorry, Dad. I was wrong. I should not have yelled at you. I hope you will forgive me." Of course I did and shared with my wife the good news that apparently our hard work at trying to teach him to apologize was paying real dividends. I knew if he could say those words to his father, then he would someday be able to say them to his wife and perhaps to his own children.

This leads me to observe that the most powerful method of teaching older children to speak the languages of apology is by your own example. When parents apologize to their children for harsh words or unfair treatment, they are doing their most effective teaching. Young children do what parents say; older children do what parents do.

The parent who reasons, "I don't want to apologize to my children because they will lose respect for me," is greatly deluded. The fact is the parent who sincerely apologizes to a child has just increased the child's respect for the parent. The child knows that what the parent did was wrong. The offense sits as a barrier between the parent and child. When the parent apologizes, the child is typically ready to forgive and the barrier is removed. Some of our finest moments are when we apologize to our children.

Another powerful method of teaching your children to speak the languages of apology is when you share examples with your children of times when you gave or received an apology. I (Arlene) had this opportunity recently when a friend asked me for a favor. I had found a new hairdresser and unbeknownst to me, my friend also went to this hairdresser.

"Would you mind telling the hairdresser that I referred you? If you do, I'll get a free haircut."

"I would be happy to do that," I answered, "except that you didn't refer me. I don't really feel comfortable saying that."

"No problem," she said.

In that moment, I lost respect for that friend because she had asked me to do something dishonest. The next morning she called.

"I feel really bad about yesterday," she said. "I didn't refer you to the hairdresser, and I was wrong to ask you to lie about that. I just wanted the free haircut. I'm sorry. Please forgive me."

I did forgive her and guess what? Her stock with me rose sharply, and my respect for her was restored. I shared that story at the dinner table with my family. We talked about how many people would not be humble enough to apologize and own up to a mistake. We praised that friend for her ability to apologize. It brought her closer as a friend and served as a vivid example of how an apology can restore trust in a relationship.

When children see adults apologizing to each other and to their kids, it helps them learn to speak the languages of apology—to *speak* the apology—not to text or instant message or post something on Facebook. If a child can practice saying "I'm sorry" in person, it will make a world of difference toward building healthy relationships in the future.

things not to say when apologizing to your kids

Do you want to use best practices for apologies that actually work? If so, omit these phrases when you are apologizing and teach your children to do the same.

Haven't you gotten over that yet?

I should be excused because I . . .

Why do you always . . . ?

If you hadn't . . .

That's just silly.

That's life.

What's the big deal?

You're acting like a baby.

You just need to get over it.

Why can't you just forget about it?

You're too sensitive. I was only joking.

Your sister (or brother) would not have been upset by what I did.

Why can't you just leave it in the past?

You just need to be tougher.

things to say when apologizing to your kids

Body language can make or break the sincerity of an apology. Be sure that you maintain eye contact, don't cross your arms defensively, listen with concern, and speak with a pleasant tone of voice. Then, choose words that do not blame others, excuse yourself, or deny responsibility.

I did it, and I have no excuse.

I'm responsible for the mistake.

I was careless.

I was insensitive.

I was rude.

My actions were not acceptable.

I will do the work to fix my mistake.

My heart aches over what I've done.

You didn't deserve that kind of treatment.

You have every right to be upset.

I know what I did was wrong.

My mistake is part of a pattern that I need to change.

I will rebuild your trust by . . .

I will try to make this up to you by . . .

I've put you in a difficult position.

I hope I haven't waited too long to say I am sorry.

Can you forgive me?

"Concentrate all your thoughts upon the work at hand. The sun's rays do not burn until brought to a focus." —ALEXANDER GRAHAM BELL

chapter seven

the A+ skill of
attention

(Arlene) have a confession. Dear reader, while I am writing on my computer, my mind often drifts to "Hmm, I wonder if anyone has sent me a message on Facebook?" "Let me check my email really fast." "What was that beep on my phone?" When I can't fight the distraction any longer, I leave the pages of this manuscript for a rabbit trail of other endless things for me to click on. Sound familiar? Keeping focused on one task in the digital age is difficult for today's adult—and it's just as hard for kids. Growing children especially need calm and quiet to develop those muscles of attention, focus, and deep thinking. Yet the screen world does not promote any of those things.

You're familiar with the term *information overload*. Picture your child's mind as a cup. When your child spends too much time looking at screens, it's like constantly aiming a water hose at that cup. His mind is unable to retain and process the current of stimuli and information. To cope with all the information, he forms the habit of moving from one thing to the next.

Tending to distractions becomes a way of life.

One college freshman sent an email about how he has struggled with Internet addiction since elementary school: "I can't focus on anything in school or at work in a deep or organized way. The only thing my mind wants to do is get back online and plug into games, news, and social media. I can't seem to concentrate on anything else."

tuning in and tuning out

"Carissa, it's time to do your homework," says her mom for the second time. Meanwhile, Carissa, eight, is playing her favorite video game on her mom's phone.

"Hello, earth to Carissa. Can you even hear me?" says her mom with a laugh.

"Just let me finish this one part. I can get to the next level," says Carissa without looking up.

Fifteen minutes later, Carissa's mom pries the phone out of Carissa's hands. Carissa sits down to do her homework. She looks at her assignment and begins to read. She fidgets and arranges the pencils in her cup. "Mom, I'm thirsty. Can I get a drink?" she asks.

After she returns from the kitchen with her drink, she sees her cat outside. He looks hungry. "Mom, I'm going to feed Romeo." With Romeo's food bowl filled up, she returns to her chair and her reading. The phone rings. "Just let it go," yells her mom from the kitchen. But Carissa shoots up from her chair to answer it. It's a telemarketer, so Carissa says, "No thank you" and hangs up.

Carissa's dad walks in the family room. "It's time for dinner."

Carissa's mom asks, "Did you finish your reading?"

"No," mumbles Carissa. "I got a little distracted."

Carissa had no trouble sitting still when she was playing her favorite game, but she couldn't sit still for long without that device to hold her attention. Have you ever marveled at how a child can sit for long stretches of time mesmerized by a screen, yet when they are presented with homework or a similar task, they cannot seem to focus for more than a few minutes? The growing presence of screens, and particularly the Internet, in daily life has changed the way we all pay attention. The Internet demands our attention and interaction more than television, radio, or newspapers ever did. We are compelled to scroll through emails, type and hit Send, and click on links for an ever-broadening menu of pages to consider. It's interactive and consuming.

The constant noise of the Internet, media, and video games is a huge barrier to creative thought and the development of deep thinking in children. A steady diet of screen time will hold your child's attention, but will it assist him in paying attention in the most important areas of his life? Screen time can condition your child to expect three things that don't always happen in real life—that what's before him will be interesting, instant, and immediately rewarding.

Screen time is interesting. There are no dull moments in the world of screens because your child can always navigate away from something if it is not interesting. Drop-down menus offer more choices. Everything is centered around what pleases the child. Even how they listen to music caters to their interests. They don't just have a CD of music they like; they have a playlist of exactly what they want to listen to. Any song they don't like gets deleted. When you can create a screen world based on your preferences, you have little desire in the real world to pay attention to anything boring, irrelevant, or unpleasant.

Screen time is instant. If you want to know the answer to "Who was Abraham Lincoln?" you don't have to open an encyclopedia or ask a teacher. You can search on your computer or phone and get the answer instantly. That ease of information is a great benefit, but it can also be a curse. Children learn that answers come easily and instantly on screens. If information requires effort to obtain, many screen-savvy kids give up. They are accustomed to instant gratification, and unfortunately that expectation spills into other areas of life, where things don't come instantly.

Screen time gives immediate rewards. When you click on a screen, you immediately get a response: A character moves, a ball is released, or a page changes to reveal something new. A child is constantly rewarded for his engagement. Children who play video games learn quickly that if they keep pressing the buttons, they will advance to the next level. Computer programmers understand that kids will play and engage indefinitely if the rewards keep coming.

Since instruction in school isn't always interesting, instantly gratifying, or rewarding, screen-driven kids enter the classroom at a disadvantage. They are not as willing to risk failure or endure boredom. Haley, a seventh grader, sat perplexed in a sewing class at school. She was supposed to cut out the material, using the pattern. She asked her teacher, "Can you cut this for me?"

Her teacher replied, "Is there something wrong with your hand?"

"No," Haley answered. "I just don't think I would be good at it."

Although she was adept with her iPad, Haley wasn't used to using scissors or working with material. She wasn't sure she would be successful in cutting the pattern, and she wasn't willing to risk making a mistake. She gave up without trying. On a screen, if you make a mistake, you can just start over without any consequences. You simply hit the Undo button, refresh a screen, or reboot. But if you cut the material wrong in the real world, you can't go back to fix it.

When a screen-driven child faces an uncertain task, she often disengages and stops paying attention. She checks out mentally when she hears something she doesn't find interesting. In the screen world, children are trained daily to get what they want, when they want it, and how they want it. That may hold their attention fast, but it doesn't sound much like the real world we are preparing our children to live in.

in praise of reading

Many parents and teachers lament the shrinking attention span of the next generation. Why has the average person's attention span dropped by 40 percent since the year 2000?[1] Part of the answer lies in the electronic devices we have given our children to benefit their lives and keep them up to date. But consider this significant caveat: the more you allow your child to use phones, tablets, and other devices, the more you foster his short attention span. Constant digital stimulation creates attention problems for children who already struggle with self-control and making healthy choices. When everything is changing every three minutes in the digital world, a child is not equipped to focus and pay attention in school. If the teacher doesn't have something fancy going on, plugged-in kids tend to get lost.

To have an idea of where children are headed in the digital age, consider this statistic about young adults between the ages of twenty-five and thirty-four. In 2008, young adults read printed works for a total of just forty-nine minutes a week, down 29 percent from 2004.[2] If today's young adult reads fewer than fifty minutes a week, what might that statistic be twenty years from now? Today's screen-driven child doesn't have the attention span to read books, yet research has repeatedly shown that access to books and reading time is a leading predictor of school success.[3]

According to the Pew Research Center, eight out of ten parents say reading print books is very important for their children.[4] Reading is a foundational and multisensory experience for every child. He touches the page while his mind processes what he is reading. At times he must force himself to stay focused on the written words. During reading time, things aren't changing every five seconds. He's following a story line and engaging in a thought process. While reading, children are learning to stay with one topic and absorb something deeply. Print reading especially strengthens attention-span muscles.

Nicholas Carr, in his book *The Shallows: What the Internet Is Doing to*

Our Brains, writes, "When we go online, we enter an environment that promotes cursory reading, hurried and distracted thinking, and superficial learning. It's possible to think deeply while surfing the Net, just as it's possible to think shallowly while reading a book, but that's not the type of thinking the technology encourages and rewards."[5]

Online reading is peppered with distracting hyperlinks and catchy headlines vying for your attention. In contrast, a book offers only one place to focus and therein offers great value for the growing child. Reading a book is a calming and relaxing activity. When a child puts down a book, he is in a good place. Contrast that to when a child puts down a tablet or phone. He is often argumentative ("Why can't I play longer?"), moody, and grumpy.

As a parent, you are able to guide your child's reading progress. For many kids, reading won't happen automatically. It must be scheduled in daily until it becomes an easy habit to maintain. Consider this comparison of three students with different reading habits.[6]

student A reads	student B reads	student C reads
20 minutes per day	5 minutes per day	1 minute per day
3,600 minutes per school year	900 minutes per school year	180 minutes per school year
1,800,000 words per year	282,000 words per year	8,000 words per year
Scores in the 90th percentile on standardized tests	Scores in the 50th percentile on standardized tests	Scores in the 10th percentile on standardized tests

If he starts reading for twenty minutes per night in kindergarten, by the end of sixth grade Student A will have read for the equivalent of sixty school days, Student B will have read for twelve school days, and Student C will have read for 3.6 days.

Which student would you like your child to be? Reading not only offers academic advantages, it will equip your child with a longer attention span and a greater capacity for concentration.

five ways to foster a love of reading for your child

Read aloud to your child. When your child is young, place him in your lap and read to him every day. Not only are you teaching him language and bonding with your child, you are creating a happy memory that will draw him to books in the future. As your kids get older, they can sit next to you while you read a book the whole family will enjoy.

Visit the library regularly. Most things in life aren't free, but the library still is. Take advantage of the vast resources of your local library. Look up favorite authors in the library catalog and request those books if you don't see them immediately available. That will give your child something to look forward to during the next trip to the library. And don't forget to pick up a book for yourself.

READING TIME FOR SCREEN TIME. Some parents have successfully helped their children embrace books by making reading a prerequisite to screen time. If your child reads for thirty minutes, she can earn thirty minutes of screen time afterward.

Find books that interest your child. What does your child enjoy—stories about ponies or biographies of baseball heroes? Look for books your child can't put down. Ask your friends with kids the same age or older for reading suggestions. Don't give up until you find a good fit for your reader.

Let them catch you reading. When your child sees you snuggled on the couch with a good book, it will encourage her to do the same. Talk to your kids about what you are reading and show them by your example that books are helpful and engaging.

screen time and attention disorders

Seven-year-old Keith returned from school on most days with red crayon colored in on his behavior chart. His mother had offered numerous awards and practically begged Keith to listen to his teacher and follow instructions. But instead of bringing home a green-colored behavior chart, Keith seemed destined to be one of those kids famous for acting up. At school he constantly talked out of turn, didn't complete his work, and never raised his hand to answer questions. Home life wasn't much better. He was disruptive during meals and aggressive toward his older sister.

His mother wondered if he had ADHD (Attention Deficit Hyperactivity Disorder) but realized he could sit for hours playing video games. There didn't seem to be anything wrong with his attention span in the digital world. However, Keith's ability to stay focused on a screen and nowhere else was actually a characteristic of attention deficit hyperactivity disorder. Many experts believe that kids with ADHD spend more time playing video games and watching television than their peers.

So is a child more fixated to screens because they have ADHD, or could the child's fixation to screens lead to ADHD? This is a complex issue, but some studies, such as a 2010 study in the journal *Pediatrics*, found viewing more television and playing more video games were linked to attention problems in schoolchildren and college students. Researchers found that children who exceeded two hours per day of screen time were one-and-a-half to two times more likely to be above average in attention problems. College students showed a similar association, suggesting that exposure to screens has lasting consequences into adulthood.[7]

The attention a child brings to a video game is unlike the concentration they need to succeed in regular life. A child like Keith can pay attention to a game fueled by frequent changes, constant rewards, new levels, points being racked up, and boosts of dopamine to the brain. When a child's brain grows accustomed to that fast pace, no wonder the real world becomes underwhelming and boring.

Kids who are struggling in school want to look for a place to succeed. Often they find that place of success in video games and virtual worlds. Children with attention disorders may retreat to the screen more often than other kids for companionship. If your child has been diagnosed with ADHD, here are a few ways you can help him navigate screen time:

Set limits on daily screen time (try two hours or less).

Don't permit screens in the bedroom.

Avoid violent video games.

Turn off the television, radio, and computer games while doing homework.

Video games can be helpful as a reward or an educational tool. But when children spend more than two hours a day playing video games and watching screens, their ability to pay attention elsewhere in life takes a big hit.

the mistake of multitasking

Suzy, eleven, plops her backpack on the table. She flips on the television to her favorite show. Pulling out her folder, she sets up what she needs for her homework. She turns on her parents' tablet to look up a definition. She glances up at the television and laughs. She continues to watch as she searches online. While Suzy is on the dictionary page, she sees an advertisement for a new movie coming out. She clicks to see more while scribbling the definition of her word in her homework folder.

Across the hall in another room, Suzy's dad, who works from home, has multiple pages open on his computer. While drafting a document, he checks his email and responds to urgent requests. The phone rings and as he listens, he scans the latest news headlines. The phone call ends, but before returning to his original document, Suzy's dad clicks on the news video to find out what the Senate is fired up about today.

Welcome to the world of multitasking. Multitasking used to be a badge of success, a shiny word to put on your resume to show your ability to manage many tasks at once. But recently, many warnings about the pitfalls of a multitasking culture are on the rise.

Multitasking reduces the quality of your work. In one experiment, students were asked to sit in a lab and complete a standard cognitive skill test. One group of subjects was not interrupted while taking the test. The other group was told they may be contacted with further instructions at any moment via text. They were interrupted twice during the exam. The interrupted group scored 20 percent less than the other group.[8] That difference is enough to bring a B-minus student down to a failing student. In another study, researchers found that workers distracted by email and phone calls suffered a fall in IQ more than twice of that found in marijuana smokers.[9]

If your child is multitasking while doing homework or other activities requiring focus, the quality of her work will suffer. When Suzy does her homework while watching television, she is prone to make errors she would catch if she weren't distracted.

Multitasking changes the way you learn. Research shows that people use different areas of the brain for learning and storing new information when they are multitasking. Brain scans of people who are distracted show activity in the striatum, a part of the brain used for learning new skills. Brain scans of people who are not distracted show activity in hippocampus, a region used for storing and recalling information.[10]

If you want your child to be able to think deeply, take away distractions such as earbuds, televisions, or computers while he is concentrating on a task. Media multitasking—using several different media simultaneously—has increased from 16 percent of media users in 1999 to 26 percent in 2005.[11] We are becoming more accustomed to using our devices all at once—the TV, texting, computer, video games, and emails. This digital immersion is changing the way your child learns.

Multitasking creates skimmers. Because multitasking trains a child to pay attention to all incoming information, he becomes adept at skimming. Otherwise, he would be overwhelmed. Think of your child's brain as a control tower. Bombarded by digital stimulus, headlines, emails, and texts, his brain keeps directing that information traffic, "Next, next, next." Multitaskers tend to search for new information instead of putting to work the older, more valuable information they already have. This translates into a child with a shallow understanding of many miscellaneous things instead of a deeper understanding of key concepts. Children who constantly multitask have a hard time sorting out the relevant from the irrelevant. Although today's English homework may be the task at hand, other things seem equally or more compelling, especially to a plugged-in child: *Look at that new game. What's that toy being advertised? Is it almost time for my favorite show?* There is little room for depth when there are so many options to sort through. Heavy multitaskers have more trouble focusing and shutting out irrelevant information.

Multitasking wastes time. Can you guess the average number of times per hour an office worker checks his email in-box? The answer is thirty times.[12] Adults are constantly toggling between tasks, which typically wastes time instead of saving it. Researchers have found it takes an average of twenty-five minutes to return to an original task after an interruption.[13]

Justin, eleven, has been sitting at the kitchen table with his homework open for more than an hour. He has reread the same math problem again and again. First, he couldn't figure out the problem, so he picked up his video game and played for a few minutes to relax. He read the problem again and decided to text his friend about it. His friend didn't understand it either; they started texting about other things. He decided to google the math problem, but he checked his favorite website first. Before long, it was time for dinner. His homework was incomplete, and he had wasted a lot of time tending to distractions.

eight ways to help your child finish homework

1. Use games or charts for rewards. Make a sticker chart where your child can place a sticker on each day that homework is done. Offer rewards for a completed week or month of homework. Create games to reward finished homework. For instance, if your child finishes homework all week, he can earn points. After fifty points, he can choose a small prize from the store.

2. HAVE A HOMEWORK SUPPLY BOX. What does your child need to complete her homework—pencils, eraser, pens, ruler, stapler, glue, tape, and scissors? Keep these supplies in one place so they are easy to find. If anything is taken out of the box, remember to replace it.

3. Know the best time for homework. Some kids like to start homework immediately after school so they can have the pleasure of playing afterward. Others need to run around for an hour after sitting at a desk for most of the day. Adjust your homework routine to what works best with your child.

4. SCHEDULE OUT BIGGER PROJECTS. When your child comes home with a large or long-term project, create a calendar to help break up the project into doable time chunks. To illustrate the value of doing a little bit at a time, tell her about a time when you procrastinated.

5. Work with a timer. If your child can complete his homework within half an hour, set a timer for thirty minutes and encourage him to finish before the timer beeps. If your child needs a longer time for homework, you can still set the timer for thirty minutes. When it beeps, take a five-minute break, and then resume the homework.

6. Offer healthy snacks. Children are often hungry after school. Avoid junk food, but offer healthy snacks like fruits or carrot sticks along with a glass of water.

7. Create an environment conducive to concentration. Is there enough light? Is the workspace uncluttered? Are the television and other electronic devices off? If your child needs to use the computer for homework, monitor usage to keep him on track.

8. Keep the same schedule every week. Children thrive in predicable schedules. You may have to adjust your homework times on different days because you have sports practice on Tuesdays and Thursdays. As long as there is a consistent routine to follow that your child understands, she will be able to make those adjustments.

attention boosters

Do you want your child to pay better attention in school? One solution isn't found in educational software, more time hitting the books, or getting a tutor. According to the American Academy of Pediatrics, *play* is essential to cognitive development in children.[14] Playtime isn't video game time; it's time to throw a Frisbee, shoot a basketball, or play hopscotch.

Being outdoors is especially rejuvenating for the minds of children and adults. A series of psychological studies revealed that after spending time close to nature in a rural setting, people exhibited greater attentiveness, stronger memory, and generally improved cognition. Their brains were calmer and sharper.

Subjects were given a series of mentally fatiguing tests designed to measure their working memory and ability to exert control over their attention. After the test, half of the group spent an hour walking through a secluded woodland park. The other half spent an hour walking along busy downtown streets. Both groups returned to take the test again. The group that spent the time in the park significantly improved their performance.[15]

The Internet cannot provide the calming experiences that nature can. There are no puffy clouds for kids to look at or peaceful streams to skip a rock on. A visit to your local park or day trip to a scenic place will help your child calm his mind, preparing him to give the attention required at school and in life.

In addition to nature, you can boost your child's ability to pay attention through nurture, namely, by eye contact. Eye contact is an essential part of strengthening your child's attention muscle. When you are talking with someone, you look at each other, which shows you have each other's attention. Every parent has said at one time or another in frustration, "Look at me when I'm talking to you!"

Many children are famous for staring at their electronic devices and little else. Teaching children to make eye contact with others helps them focus their attention on the person at hand. When you insist upon eye contact and give it generously, you help your child pay attention relationally to others and increase his level of empathy.

In our society and at home, children see modeled a primary relationship with screens and a lack of eye contact with people. In marriage, often the complaint is, "He says he's listening, but he's always watching TV or he's got the computer on." Or it could be a husband trying to get eye contact from his wife while she's on social media. Technically the spouse may be listening, but maintaining eye contact demonstrates that he or she is paying attention.

In this digital age, so many things vie for your attention and the attention of your child. The ding of a new text message. Streaming videos. The next level of a video game. Dozens of new emails. Both adults and children must learn to pay attention to the important things of life, even in the absence of stimulus, rewards, or entertainment.

What William James wrote in the 1800s is relevant for today: "The faculty of voluntarily bringing back a wandering attention, over and over again, is the very root of judgment, character, and will." Your child's ability to pay attention is not only an academic concern. It's a matter of the heart.

"Shyness is fueled in part by so many people spending huge amounts of time alone, isolated on email, in chat rooms, which reduces their face-to-face contact with other people." —PHILIP ZIMBARDO

chapter eight

screen time and
shyness

Now you understand the five A+ skills your child needs to succeed relationally: affection, appreciation, anger management, apology, and attention. In this next section of the book, we are going to answer those nagging questions many parents have expressed about the impact of screen time on family life.

Seated next to other parents, Nikki pulled out a magazine from her purse to read while waiting for her daughter to finish ballet practice. Before reading, she decided to introduce herself to the mom next to her.

"Hi, I'm Nikki. What's your name?"

"Oh, nice to meet you," said the other lady who was sitting next to a boy who looked about ten. "I'm Grace, and this is my son, Peter." She gestured toward Peter and turned toward him. "Peter, this is Miss Nikki."

Peter continued to look down at his video game. His mother's words didn't faze him. After pausing a moment, his mom said sheepishly, "Sorry about that. Peter is very shy. He's always been that way."

Although Peter was adept at making friends at school and had no trouble giving presentations in his fourth grade class, he had always acted shy with adults. His mother had never forced him to engage with her friends because she thought Peter was timid and would eventually come around on his own.

Kids like Peter can easily hide behind electronic screens to avoid interactions with others that seem unpleasant or unnecessary. Studies show increasing numbers of young people who report being shy. Many experts believe this rising number is partially due to the social isolation that comes with being digitally connected. Video games, searching websites, emailing, texting, and instant messaging are done alone, in private, without looking at anyone else. Plugged-in kids aren't getting as much experience with nonverbal communication and face-to-face interaction.

In one study, about half of the kids in America described themselves as being shy, but only 12 percent of those surveyed met the criteria for social phobia.[1] Most of the kids surveyed are like Peter; they are not truly shy. They can be taught to interface with others with relative ease if we can just get them to put down their screens.

shyness: what it is and what it isn't

When referring to shyness, we are talking about a child who is nervous and uncomfortable meeting and talking to people. Shy children don't adapt as well as their peers in the classroom or playground because they are timid in the company of others. The longer a child practices the pattern of avoiding new people and withdrawing from social settings, the more of a hindrance this will be in adult life.

However, do not confuse being shy with being quiet. If one of your children is the life of the party, but the other one hardly says a word in public, it doesn't mean your quieter child is shy. Outgoing, extroverted, talkative children are the objects of much praise. But quieter, introverted children bring strengths such as being great listeners and analytic thinkers.

If you are wondering what is healthy and what is unhealthy when it comes to a child who is quiet and reserved, consider these characteristics:

healthy	unhealthy
Makes eye contact with others	Avoids eye contact with others
Polite	Rude, unresponsive
Content	Dissatisfied
Generally exhibits good behavior	Has behavior problems
People are comfortable with him	People are not comfortable with him

Don't think of your child as shy just because he is quiet. Maybe he won't raise his hand in class, but he'll discuss a subject in a small group. It's okay if your child is more reserved than others. And even if your child is nervous and afraid of people and new situations, avoid labeling him as shy.

When a child hears over and over that he is shy, it gives him an excuse for not developing social skills. A child can say, "Oh, I'm just shy," giving him a pass to skip politeness and conversation. For some children, being shy becomes very convenient.

You don't have to mold your reserved child into becoming a social butterfly. You simply want to teach him how to participate in life and enjoy the company of others. Introverted and extroverted children have this in common: they all have to learn what's appropriate when interacting with people.

creating a new normal

Remember how ten-year-old Peter avoided meeting that mom at ballet practice? There can certainly be a reticence on the part of children to open up and get to know someone who is talking to their parents. Adults can be intimidating. As parents, we must remember that children will do what we teach them to do. If we teach our children from a young age to look an adult in the eyes and ask questions, we are teaching them a valuable skill. They become comfortable with talking with adults because we have taught them how to do so. Children who feel threatened or nervous when talking with others can practice inside and outside of the home until they experience a new norm of interacting with people. Children who are disinterested can be taught about common courtesy.

The same thing is true in teaching kids to interact with other kids. The next time you are in a social setting and you see a child alone, you can say to your son, "Look at Paul. He's all by himself. Why don't you go over and talk with him? All the other kids are playing, and maybe he thinks that nobody cares about him. Why don't you invite him to join in the game?" In so doing, you are teaching your son to be proactive to befriend others.

I (Arlene) was reserved as a child. When my parents started attending a church, I didn't want to be separated from them, so I refused to go into the children's room with the other elementary school kids. After many months of sitting next to my parents in the main service, my mother decided to give me a little pep talk.

"You are going to try the children's program soon," she said. "When you go into the room, look for the other kids who are by themselves. They are probably just as nervous as you are about being there. You can sit next to them and ask them questions about what they like to do and about their family. If you look for people who need a friend, you won't be lonely yourself."

It was hard at first to overcome that nervousness to talk with a child I didn't know. But before long, I learned to say hi to girls who were sitting alone. I became more and more comfortable talking to other kids, and now some thirty years later, I still follow my mom's advice when I'm in a room filled with people I don't know.

You can help your son or daughter create a new normal when it comes to interacting with people. Instruct your child to focus on the other person instead of himself when he feels nervous. Resist the temptation to speak for your child when you are together. If there is an awkward pause, give your child plenty of time to engage instead of quickly rescuing your child.

If your child is using an electronic device when a person begins talking to him, teach your child to put down the device, look at the person, and smile. People first. Phones, tablets, or video games second. Technology does offer some benefits for the shy child. A girl may be uncomfortable speaking in a large group, but she can type her opinion from the privacy of her living room and post it for hundreds of kids to see. She may role-play in a virtual world and learn something that may help her in a real-world situation with friends.

But use discernment with online time. Children who have trouble with shyness may retreat too much to the screen for electronic companionship. The most powerful way to overcome shyness is to practice interacting with others in daily life—at home, school, sports practice, or the grocery-store line. If a child is spending hours online every day, he doesn't gain experience with other people because he's spending most of his free time alone with screens.

practice, practice, practice

When it comes to learning a new skill like hitting a baseball or playing the piano, you know the saying "Practice makes perfect." The role of practice is just as important when learning positive social skills. Consider your home as the dress rehearsal. It's a safe place where your children can practice making conversation for common social settings they will experience.

Begin by explaining how your child will benefit from acting friendly even when he would rather withdraw. Some benefits may be having more fun, making good friends, or enjoying school and social activities more. Share how becoming friendly has helped you in your life. Maybe you had to overcome shyness in your career to become a teacher or a salesperson.

Here are a few scenarios to practice at home with your child:

Successful playdates. Pretend you are a friend coming over to play with your son. "What should we play?" you ask. Have your son pick five fun activities to choose from (things like board games, Legos, soccer, or basketball). Play for a few minutes together, and talk about how much fun it will be to have a friend over. Then make it really happen by inviting a good boy your son feels comfortable around. Make screens off-limits and be sure to serve an extra delicious snack.

Playground fun. Go outside and pretend you are at your child's school playground. Walk her through what happens at recess. Ask, "What do you do when you first get to the playground?" Suggest that she look for a friend from class or another girl who is standing alone. How would she go about joining a group of girls who were playing? What if they say there's no room for her? Run through different scenarios and how she can respond. Listen to her concerns or anxiety about recess and playing with others. Role-play the situations to help her practice interacting with her classmates.

Navigating the classroom. Have your child sit at a table as you pretend to be the teacher. Ask a question, and have your son raise his hand and tell you the answer. Let him know he doesn't have to raise his hand every time in class, but that it would be a good goal to raise his hand once a week. Stress the importance of making eye contact with his teacher. If your child has to present something to the whole class, practice many times at home in front of siblings and plenty of stuffed animals.

Meeting adults. You can make this activity more fun by putting on a costume like a hat or jacket. Practice the introduction as you pretend to be the new adult. "Joy, this is Mrs. Davis." Have your child look you in the eyes and say, "It's nice to meet you, Mrs. Davis." Go one step further and teach your child to ask the new acquaintance a question: "How are you today?" or "What do you do for your job?"

Giving and receiving compliments. Pretend to be a friend, coach, or teacher, and give your child a compliment like "You did a very good job on your drawing." Have your child practice looking you in the eyes and saying, "Thank you." Encourage your child not to mumble his thanks but to say it clearly and enthusiastically. Then have your child practice giving a compliment to you. Challenge your child to compliment one person that day and report back to you on how it goes.

Asking for help. This will be an easy one for you to act out. Pretend you are busy at your desk. Have your child interrupt you with an urgent need. You want to teach your child to assert herself and speak up if she has a legitimate need that can't wait at school or other places. Explain the difference between an urgent, important need and something that can wait. If your child is being bullied at school or elsewhere, she needs confidence to speak up and tell someone. You can role-play that scenario before it happens so she will know what to do if it ever does.

Reading nonverbals. Successful communication consists of both words and nonverbal cues. Screens can't teach a child the nuances of body language or facial expressions. But you can act out different facial expressions to quiz your child. As you make different faces (sad, angry, happy, etc.), ask your child to name the feeling. You can thumb through a magazine together and identify the different emotions the people pictured are displaying. What might they be feeling by the way they look? What does their body language tell you?

The more you practice these social skills at home, the more comfortable your child will feel using them outside of the home. You can then expose your child to a wider range of experiences such as:

- Going to the library for story time
- Joining a group such as Girl Scouts or Boy Scouts
- Asking a salesperson at the bookstore for help finding a book
- Going to the zoo with another family
- Ordering food at a restaurant
- Talking with the clerk at the grocery store

Another thing you can do is provide some incentive for your child to come out of his shell. You can assign points to certain activities and then have a celebration or prize for points earned. For example:

1 point for talking to a friend at recess

3 points for giving eye contact when meeting an adult

5 points for having a friend over for a playdate

10 points for joining an afterschool club

rejection, bullies, and bad hair days

Six-year-old Wendy came home in tears—again. Since changing to a new school three weeks earlier, she still hadn't been able to make friends. She was shy, and the move was especially hard on her. Today at lunch she had made a brave attempt to sit next to some girls from class, but they looked up and said, "Sorry, we don't have any more space at this table." She quietly found another place to sit in the cafeteria as she fought back tears.

Since Wendy wasn't having much success in the friend department, she stopped trying to initiate conversations at recess. She became more withdrawn in the classroom, often avoiding eye contact with her classmates and teacher. At home, she started watching a lot more television after school.

Five Things Not to Say to Your Reserved Child

1. Don't be shy.
2. Don't worry; they won't bite.
3. Don't just sit there. Say something!
4. Cat got your tongue?
5. Why can't you be outgoing like your sister?

Eric, eleven, loved playing soccer, but he dreaded going to practice. One of his teammates, Luke, twelve, constantly made fun of him. He'd say things like, "If you want to score, don't pass the ball to Eric" and "Who taught you to play? A bunch of girls?" Eric didn't tell his parents about the bullying. Instead he threw himself into his video games where he could be the one calling the shots.

When kids like Wendy and Eric have trouble in social settings, it's easier than ever to retreat to the safety of screens. If you feel left out, just fiddle with a smartphone or play a video game. You'll look busy, occupied, and important. Being with screens is a lot easier than being with people. Screens don't care if you say or do the right thing. They will not judge your comments or behavior. You don't have to put your best foot forward or risk embarrassment or rejection. Your tablet doesn't care if you're having a bad hair day and it won't ever make fun of you. You can simply be with a game or television program that makes you feel connected with very little effort.

If a shy child spends three, four, or five hours a day watching television or playing video games, what is that child missing out on? Healthy human interactions like sitting around chatting with family, shopping for groceries, shooting hoops in the driveway, or playing games with a sibling. Those types of activities help a child interact with greater ease with people, not only within the family unit but in general. On the other hand, screen time can further ostracize a child and reinforce negative behavior. According to the Mayo Clinic, watching excessive amounts of television at age four is linked with bullying at ages six through eleven.[2]

If a child is mostly connected to computers and video game devices, how is he going to learn to adapt to people instead of withdrawing or acting out? When a shy child has strong, personal connections at home, it gives him a great advantage when he has to deal with bullies or rejection. A mom or dad can lovingly guide him through the harsh things kids can say.

mealtime grace

There is a built-in time every day to connect to your child's heart—and it's triggered by her stomach. Research shows that eating meals as a family benefits children greatly. Young people whose families routinely eat meals together spend more time on homework and reading for pleasure. They are more likely to eat nutritious food and less likely to engage in future substance use, sexual intercourse, or suicidal tendencies.[3]

What you do during the mealtime is hugely important. Is the television on? Are you quickly gobbling your food to get out the door? If so, you are missing out on the value of family mealtime. Having a meal together is a time for *conversation*. These sacred moments around the table can draw out your shy child. If it's dinnertime, you can ask your child questions like "What did you enjoy most today?" and "What was hardest for you to do today?" It's amazing what you can learn sitting around the table if you will listen. (You can find more table talk questions at 5Love-Languages.com.)

Remember to put your phones on vibrate, and don't pick up during mealtime. Turn the television and radio off unless it's just soft music in the background. Don't allow the interruptions of screens to compromise your quality time together. Show your children that dinner is not only a time to eat, it's a time to talk.

With competing schedules, it can be challenging to find a common time when every member of the family can sit down for a meal. One son might have football practice while another is taking piano lessons, and you are running around town like a professional shuttle service. I (Gary) remember when we had to bounce back and forth from eating early to eating late because of the kids' schedule or my schedule. But we all knew that family dinner was important, and we strove to make it work.

We suggest making it a family goal to eat seven or more meals together a week. Depending on what works with your family's schedule, that might be dinner every night, or most meals on the weekend with a few meals during the week. There might be a night when you have to eat fast food in the car on the way to the game, but make that the exception, not the rule.

Before leaving this topic of mealtime, we need to touch on the importance of good nutrition and the self-esteem of your child. When a child is a healthy body weight and able to engage in active pursuits like sports or playground games, it gives him a boost of self-confidence. Unfortunately, more than one-third of children and adolescents are overweight or obese. This health crisis puts children at risk for diseases that are unthinkable for the young: cardiovascular disease, prediabetes, bone and joint problems, and sleep apnea, to name a few.[4]

Children hooked on screen time are not only sedentary, but they are also being fed a stream of advertising that increases their desire for unhealthy foods. Screen-time kids are exposed to 5,000 to 10,000 food ads per year, most of them for fast food and junk food.[5] Watching television or playing video games at night also hinders sleep. A child can easily step into a vicious cycle of watching television or playing video games, not exercising, eating junk food, sleeping poorly, and gaining weight. These are destructive patterns for any child, and for the shy child it can be particularly debilitating as it leads to further isolation.

A shy child who already is uncomfortable in social settings will become even more nervous if she is dealing with weight issues. What you serve on the family dinner table—both in calories and conversation—will make a lasting impact on your child's well-being.

Remember, you are not trying to create an extrovert or coax a quiet child to become something he is not. Instead you want to help your child to relax in the presence of others and to connect through meaningful relationships. Social contact is a core human need. Interacting with screens more than people can foster an unhealthy pattern of isolation. But you can fight against that one meal at a time, one conversation at a time, until your child finds comfort in the presence of others.

"The current explosion of digital technology not only is changing the way we live and communicate but is rapidly and profoundly altering our brains."

—DR. GARY SMALL

chapter nine

screen time and
the brain

When my (Arlene's) children watch television, they are riveted by what is happening on the screen. When my husband walks into the room and sees them with eyes transfixed and bodies motionless, he declares, "Quick! Turn off the video before their brains are sucked out of their heads!"

No doubt you have seen your kids glued to a screen. Although you know their brains are intact, you probably have wondered what all that technology *is* doing to their brains. Moving images are extraordinarily stimulating to the brain, whether on a flat-screen television or a smartphone. A child's growing brain is particularly sensitive, and it is increasingly exposed to new technology.

When a baby is born, he comes into the world equipped with a hundred billion neurons. During the first three years of life, these overabundant neurons are active, building connections to each other. The extra neurons are pruned back around the age of three. It's like the pruning of a tree; by cutting back the weak connections, the strong ones flourish.

Using MRI scans, neuroscientists have mapped out brain growth in individual children and teenagers. Frontal brain circuits, which control attention, grow fastest between the ages of three to six. The second spurt of synapse formation happens in the brain just before puberty (roughly age eleven in girls, age twelve in boys). Then there's a pruning back of neurons again in adolescence.[1]

Some experts theorize this is a particularly important time in development that can impact a child for the rest of his life. Dr. Jay Giedd from the National Institute of Mental Health says, "Our leading hypothesis . . . is the 'use it or lose it' principle. If a teen is doing music or sports or academics, those are the cells and connections that will be hardwired. If they're lying on the couch or playing video games or [watching] MTV, those are the cells and connections that are going to survive."[2]

Digital natives are spending an average of eight hours a day on screens. If your child is one of them, ask yourself: "What type of brain cells and connections will be shaping his future?"

your child's brain on technology

Dr. Gary Small, head of UCLA's memory and aging research center, conducted a fascinating experiment to demonstrate how people's brains change in response to Internet use. He took a dozen experienced web surfers and a dozen nonusers and scanned their brains as they performed searches on Google. The computer savvy group showed broad brain activity in the left-front part of the brain known as the dorsolateral prefrontal cortex, while the novices showed little, if any, activity in this area. Their brains look very different when searching the Internet. But when both groups read straight text in a book, the brain scans of the two groups were alike.

The novices were then instructed to spend just one hour a day searching the Internet for five days. Following that period, the test was repeated.

The new scans showed the novice group now had the same brain activity in the prefrontal cortex as the computer savvy group when searching Google. In only five hours of Internet use, this group had rewired their brains.[3]

Parents who are concerned their young children will be left behind if they don't board the technology train can take comfort in this experiment. It doesn't take the brain a long time to learn how to use technology. If you had your child on the Internet for five hours like the group in the experiment, no doubt they would quickly become proficient in web searches, instant messaging, video games, and tweeting.

But what about the opposite scenario? If your child grows up with screens throughout preschool and elementary school, can he take that wired brain and produce the concentration required during a classroom lecture? Can his brain readily produce empathy for a friend or read a long passage with comprehension? These skills are much harder to pick up in a short period of time.

With increased screen use, the neural circuits that control the more traditional learning methods used for reading, writing, and sustained concentration are neglected. Jeremy, eleven, spends his time after school and soccer practice playing video games. He doesn't bother to learn his vocabulary words because he knows spell-check can fix the words and texting doesn't require spelling.

Isn't it interesting that the chief technology officer of eBay sends his children to a nine-classroom school where technology is totally omitted? So do employees of digital giants like Google, Apple, Yahoo, and Hewlett-Packard. No computers and no screens to be found.[4] Bill Gates only allowed his daughters on the Internet forty-five minutes a day, including video games. He also waited until they turned thirteen to permit having a cellphone.[5]

Children who grow up on screens become wired to use their gadgets to communicate instead of face-to-face-interaction with people. Dr.

Gary Small says, "The pathways for human interaction and communication weaken as customary one-on-one people skills atrophy."[6] Texting and social media work to supplement communication, but when they are the total sum of contact, your child is missing out.

Kids love the words *I*, *me*, and *my*. The young brain is not naturally empathetic toward others. Empathy must be learned and screen time often works against that. When you are physically with someone, you can see their expression change when his or her feelings are hurt. You can't see or feel that emotion online. Videos that embarrass other children can become the next sensation that everyone is sharing with little consideration to the feelings of the people involved. When a child spends too much time with electronics, he can become detached from the feelings of others. Online searches often go awry, exposing your child's brain to graphic images and inappropriate content.

To be fair, there are benefits of screen time for the brain. Using the Internet equips a child's brain for rapid-fire cyber searches. The brain muscles being developed have to do with quick decision making, visual acuity, and multitasking. A child who plays video games may be able to see something in his peripheral vision that a nongamer doesn't notice. Gamers can excel in visual motor tasks like using a joystick, tracking objects, or visual searches.

But are these benefits important enough to sacrifice in other areas of brain development such as reading, writing, sustained concentration, and empathy?

twenty-first-century reading

Invented in 1455, Gutenberg's press would become one of the most influential inventions in history. The print age delivered knowledge to anyone who was willing to learn how to read. Reading books strengthened the muscles of reasoning, logic, and order. The left brain became the dominant hemisphere, with many readers excelling in fields such as science. Experiments have revealed the brains of the literate differ from the brains of the illiterate in the way they understand language, process visual signals, reason, and form memories.[7]

Centuries later, our children are no longer reading the same way they used to. I (Arlene) was shocked to thumb through a New England Primer dated 1777, considered the most influential school textbook in the history of American education. The primer was used for students just beginning to read; it would be equivalent to a first grade text.

Could your child read these sentences in first grade?

Acumen denotes quickness of perception.
Molasses is the syrup which drains from sugar when it is cooling.
A tribunal is a court for deciding causes.

Or how about these spelling words, written in syllables:

Tem per a ture
Pa rish ion er
Com mi ser ate
Mis cel la ne ous

Not exactly like today's first grade vocabulary, is it? What has happened to diminish the intellectual abilities of children? There was the invention of radio, cinema, phonograph, and television, which introduced a new world of entertainment to a child. But until recently, the written word was still found only in books. Through the electronic revolution, words are now found on desktop computers, tablets, and smartphones. The Internet is our new medium of choice to find, store, and share information.

Nicolas Carr writes, "The world of the screen, as we're already coming to understand, is a very different place from the world of the page. A new intellectual ethic is taking hold. The pathways in our brains are once again being rerouted."[8] For example, kids and teens today don't necessarily read a page from left to right and from top to bottom. They might instead skip around, scanning for interesting information. The Internet has trained them to read like this. Online reading is nonlinear, peppered with hyperlinks to jump to, with no fundamental beginning, middle, and end.

Just pick up a popular magazine for adults or kids, and you'll notice this shift to shorter articles, bigger photos, large headlines, quick summaries, blurbs, and pull quotes. There's nothing wrong with skimming and browsing magazines, the Internet, or books. But there is something wrong if skimming has become the dominant way for your child to read.

Traditional book readers show activity in brain regions associated with language, memory, and visual processing while reading, but they don't display much activity in the prefrontal regions tied with decision making and problem solving. However, Internet users show extensive activity across all those decision-making and problem-solving brain regions when they scan web pages. Deep reading is difficult online because the brain must evaluate links, decide where to navigate, and process distractions like advertisements. All of this pulls the brain from understanding the text at hand. Our brains online are busy making decisions and navigating through distractions, but they are not engaged in focused learning.

the reward center

Bella, five, pushes a button on the remote control and receives an image that makes her laugh. You see the smile on her face, but what is going on

Young Brains on Screens[9]

By the time a child is . . .

Two years old: More than 90 percent of all American children have an online history (such as having their baby photo posted), and 38 percent have used a mobile device.

Five years old: More than 50 percent regularly interact with a computer or tablet.

Seven years old: Most regularly play video games.

A teenager: Will text an average of 3,400 times per month and will spend more time with media than with parents or teachers.

in her brain? The *nucleus accumbens*, the pleasure center of the brain, is in charge of controlling every experience of pleasure. As Bella watches a cartoon, the neurotransmitter dopamine carries a signal of pleasure to that pleasure center. Bella feels good while she's watching television. That's partially why it's difficult to pry her away for homework or dinner.

As children go for more pleasure by watching more television or playing more video games, they are pushing the dopamine level in their brain higher and higher. But as the brain's pleasure system is overused, the feeling of pleasure is diminished. The thirty minutes of video games that used to thrill a child now doesn't produce the same joy. So she seeks to play longer or find a more stimulating game. She's looking for that fresh squirt of dopamine.

Pleasure, in the right amounts, is a very good thing, but in excess it's detrimental to your child. Just compare the difference between taking a family vacation to Disneyland to living at the theme park for a year. Pleasure *can* be overdone. Dr. Archibald Hart and Dr. Sylvia Hart Frejd write in their book *The Digital Invasion,*

> Many of our Internet behaviors, such as gambling or gaming on the Internet, or even Facebooking, can do as much damage to the pleasure center as any powerful drug. The pleasure center can become so flooded that only the "big" stimulants can get a message to the pleasure center. Little, ordinary pleasures are ignored because they do not have the power to overcome the flooding . . . What this all means is that the thrills of our digital world, if abused, can be as addicting as any drug and rob you of the simple joys of life.[10]

what is screen addiction?

It's a relatively new term but one that is increasingly used by physicians: *screen addiction.* One study asked a thousand students in ten countries to stop using technology and media for just one day. At the end of that twenty-four-hour period, many students repeatedly used the word *addiction.* One student said, "I was itching, like a crackhead, because I could not use my phone." Others could not complete the one-day technology fast. Most said they missed their phone because it was their source of connection and comfort.[11]

In China, Taiwan, and Korea, Internet Addiction Disorder is on the rise, with as many as 30 percent of teens in these countries considered addicted. In South Korea, most teenagers participate in gaming centers. Sitting in rows of small cubbies and computers, teens and young adults settle in for long periods to play multiplayer computer games for an hourly fee. Teens and students in their twenties often play through the night and then go to school or work exhausted.

In extreme cases, computer addiction has turned deadly. A twenty-eight-year-old man in Korea played for fifty hours, taking just a few breaks. After he collapsed in an Internet café, he was rushed to the hospital where he died shortly after, presumably of heart failure due to exhaustion.[12] In response to the alarming problem of gaming addiction, South Korea introduced a law that prohibits teens age sixteen and younger from playing online games between midnight and 6:00 a.m. Hundreds of private hospitals and clinics throughout the country have opened to treat Internet Addiction Disorder.

Parents in America are wise to heed the warnings of South Korea. It's estimated that 95 to 97 percent of American youth are playing video games of one type or another.[13] The important questions to ask are "How long does your child play?" and "What type of games is he playing?" Many psychologists are concerned that extensive computer game playing in children may lead to long-term changes in the brain's circuitry that resemble the effects of substance dependence. Kids addicted to gaming can't resist the urge to play, even if it interrupts basic hygiene, eating, sleeping, homework, and relating to family or friends.

Puzzle games such as Tetris or Solitaire are not nearly as addicting as first-person shooter games. Even more addicting than the shooter games are MMORPGs (Massively Multiplayer Online Role-Playing Games) in which a very large number of players interact with each other within a virtual game world. Be aware of the risk of addiction inherent in the games your child is choosing. Not all games are created equal.

Brain imaging results suggest that violent video games can directly alter brain activity in as little as one week of playing. Researchers took a group of young men, ages eighteen to twenty-nine years old, who had little to no experience with violent video games. Half the participants played a shooting game for ten hours over the next week and then not at all during the second week. The other group didn't play video games at all. The young men who played video games showed less activation in portions of the brain responsible for controlling emotional regulation and aggressive behavior than the other group of nongamers. This pattern was found again at the end of the second week, even though the group had stopped playing the violent video games. Only one week of playing for ten hours was enough to change something in the brain.[14]

your child's plastic brain

Your child's brain may not turn to mush, but you could say it's made out of plastic. Brain plasticity refers to the brain's ability to change and adapt. Scientists and doctors used to believe brain anatomy was fixed after childhood, but recent studies have proved that adult brains can change in response to new information, behavior, or environment.

In the late 1990s, British researchers scanned the brains of sixteen London cab drivers. They found that the taxi drivers' posterior hippocampus, the part of the brain responsible for spatial navigation was much larger than normal. In addition, the longer the cab driver had been on the job, the larger his posterior hippocampus was. Even in adulthood, their brains had changed.[15]

Old brains can be taught new tricks, but it's easier to learn those tricks when you're young. Your child's brain is capable of learning math, reading, foreign language, music, and more. As a parent, you can mold your child's brain in a positive way by balancing screen time with reading, sports, and other activities.

My (Arlene's) son, Ethan, nine, loves to read. We have filled our home with biographies of heroes because we want Ethan to fill his brain with stories of courage and moral character. He's gobbled up books about Winston Churchill, Eric Liddell, Corrie ten Boom, Douglas MacArthur, and the like. When I was visiting his public school, the librarian pulled me aside and told me this story.

"I was reading the book *Yertle the Turtle* by Dr. Seuss to Ethan's third grade class," the librarian said. "The story is about Yertle, the king of the pond who stands on his subjects in an attempt to reach higher than the moon. I told the class that Dr. Seuss had modeled the character of the king turtle after a famous world leader. Could anyone guess who?"

Ethan's hand shot up. "Hitler," he answered.

The librarian was amazed. Ethan was right. In her many years of being a librarian, he was the first third grader who had answered it correctly.

She went on to tell me that some sixth graders can't make that kind of connection. That incident made a big impression on the librarian—and on me too. I saw the fruit of having a reader instead of an expert video gamer. Ethan's brain is plastic, and I have the opportunity to mold it on purpose.

peace of mind

Kurt and Leslie have two children, ages nine and eleven. Their good friends have children the same age who have televisions in their rooms. As a result, Kurt and Leslie's kids were constantly asking if they could have televisions too. But the answer was always no. Kurt and Leslie believed that too much digital stimulation was bad for the brain.

Many experts would agree. When children overuse technology, the constant stimulation of the brain causes the stress hormone cortisol to rise. Too much cortisol can inhibit a child from feeling calm and comforted. Dr. Archibald Hart says, "A part of cortisol's function is to block the tranquility receptors so as to make you more anxious and prepare you to deal with an emergency. Only, it isn't a real emergency but instead a game-induced emergency. This loss of tranquility can lead to more serious anxiety disorders."[16]

If your child is spending hours playing video games, texting, or engaging in social media, cortisol is flooding her brain. To lower your child's stress level, practice these four things in your family to experience peace of mind instead.

Downtime. After a good workout, physical muscles need rest to recover. The same is true for the brain. It's not that the brain gets tired, but it needs time between tasks to process and consolidate information. This free "brain time" for kids is often eaten up by screen time. Your child's brain needs to be idle from time to time.

Restricted electronic use. Without enforced limits, a child can easily spend hours moving from screen to screen. One television episode turns into two. A short video game break turns into one hour of playing. Christy, a fourth grade teacher, estimates her students spend at least half of their free time after school playing video games. She wishes her students had screen-time limits at home and more reading and physical activities instead.

Physical exercise. Exercise affects your child's growing brain in many positive ways. It increases heart rate (which pumps more oxygen to the brain), reduces cortisol, and burns off adrenaline. Studies show that kids who exercise regularly get higher grades, have better concentration, and sleep well.[17] Physical activity releases brain chemicals that are natural stress fighters.

Sleep. Certain stages of sleep are needed to cement what your child learned during the day. That learning doesn't take place if your child is sleep-deprived. The following day, a sleepy child is unable to focus and pay attention to new material. It's a vicious cycle, but it can be remedied with a few sleep strategies. Set a consistent bedtime for your child, and make her room dark, quiet, and comfortable. Don't have any screens in the bedroom because staring at a bright screen before bedtime keeps kids awake. Turn off the television, computer, or tablet one hour before bedtime to avoid stimulating adrenaline and preventing sleep. Remember also the secret weapon of exercise—the more vigorous the activity, the bigger the sleep benefits.

If you haven't been practicing these habits, it's not too late to begin. As long as your child lives under your roof, you can make healthy adjustments starting today. A father named Jerry, who attended one of my (Gary's) conferences, had two children, a twenty-two-year-old boy and a nineteen-year-old girl. Although he set time limits for computer and television use, he said he would do things differently now. "I would not have allowed much of what I allowed if I could do it over again with my kids. Looking back, I know the advertisements and programs they watched were not good role models. We could have spent more time together as a family." Jerry's children are grown. It's too late for him to exchange that screen time for something more valuable.

But it's not too late for you. Neurosurgeon Ben Carson said, "Don't let anyone turn you into a slave. You're a slave if you let the media tell you that sports and entertainment are more important than developing your brain."[18] Your child and his billion plus brain cells are waiting to be nourished and developed—not by screens but by you as a parent.

"I dream of a day when all children can grow up in homes filled with love and security, where their developing energies can be channeled to learning and serving rather than craving and searching for the love they did not receive from home."

—DR. GARY CHAPMAN

screen time and the
love languages

TMOT. TAU. TCOY. Sometimes it may seem that you and your child are speaking different languages. These text abbreviations stand for "Trust me on this," "Thinking about you," and "Take care of yourself." Communication is possible when you understand the code, but it's awfully hard without it.

I (Gary) have been teaching people for decades about the five love languages, which are physical touch, words of affirmation, quality time, gifts, and acts of service. These love languages are a code to help you understand how your child receives love. I'll never forget the couple Brad and Emily, who approached me at my "The Marriage You've Always Wanted" seminar. They were concerned about their son, Caleb, eight, who was struggling in school, acting aggressive toward other kids, and clinging to his teacher. Prior to the third grade, he had been an above-average learner, happy, and independent.

I asked Brad and Emily if their lifestyle had changed in the past year. Brad's sales job kept him out making calls two nights a week. On the other weeknights at home, he caught up on emails and texts. He used to go to football games with Caleb on the weekends, but he hadn't done that in a year. Emily had switched from working part-time to full-time, which meant she no longer picked Caleb up from school.

After learning about the love languages, they agreed that Caleb's primary love language was *quality time.* They realized they had not spent a great deal of time with their son in the past several months. I encouraged Brad to build time with Caleb into his schedule and for Emily to look for ways to spend time with him like she used to before working full time.

About two years later, Brad and Emily attended another seminar and waited to give me an encouraging report. They both smiled and said, "Caleb's doing great. We consciously gave him lots of quality time. Within two or three weeks, really, we saw a dramatic change in his behavior. His teacher asked us to come in, and we were worried. But this time she wanted to ask what we had done to bring about such a change in Caleb."

This couple learned to speak their son's love language, to say "I love you" in a way he could understand. In raising children, everything hinges on the love relationship between the parent and child. Nothing works well if a child's love needs are not met. Only the child who feels genuinely loved and cared for can have successful, healthy relationships.

Every child has an emotional tank, a place of emotional strength that fuels him through the challenging days of childhood and adolescence. Speaking these love languages to your child fills up this emotional tank. When your child's tank is full of your unconditional love, it's much easier to have conversations about and set limits for screen time. But when your child feels neglected in his preferred love languages, screen time can further erode your relationship.

So how does technology impact the way you express love to your child? Raising emotionally healthy children is an increasingly difficult task in this digital world that demands so much of our attention. In this chapter, you will find a brief explanation of each love language. To learn more about the love languages, we recommend you read *The 5 Love Languages of Children.*

love language #1: physical touch

Samantha is a fifth grader whose family recently moved to a new community. "It's been hard this year, moving and having to make new friends," said Samantha. When she was asked if she ever felt as if her parents didn't love her because they took her away from her old town, she said, "Oh no, I know they love me, because they always give me lots of extra hugs and kisses."

Like many children, Samantha's love language is physical touch; those touches make her feel secure and let her know Mom and Dad love her. The language of touch isn't confined to a hug or a kiss but includes any kind of physical contact. Even when you are busy, you can often gently touch your child on her back, arm, or shoulder. Although this love language is easy to express, studies indicate that many parents touch their children only when it is necessary: when they are dressing or undressing them, putting them in the car, or carrying them to bed. It seems many parents are unaware of how much their children need to be touched and how easily they can use this means to keep their children's emotional tanks filled with love.

Bob has two children in elementary school and one in preschool. When the two older kids were younger, Bob would often put them in his lap and read them a bedtime story. Reading together builds a sense of oneness, a sense of love for kids. But life got busier and, nowadays, the older kids read on their own. The youngest daughter, Lisa, four, is used to reading children's books on an eReader. Bob rarely puts Lisa on his lap to read *Goodnight Moon*. She sits by herself on the couch reading with her device.

An electronic reader may save space, trees, and inconvenience, but using one with kids short-circuits something important—physical touch between a parent and child. Sure a parent can put a child on his lap and read an eReader or play a video game together on a tablet. But typically, when a child is engaged with a screen, he or she is not touching a parent. He's not being held in a lap. He's not sitting close enough to touch Mom's or Dad's leg. When family members get used to engaging with screens, they lose the physical touch that should be a normal dynamic in a healthy family.

If your child's primary love language is touch, you will know it. They will be jumping on you, poking you, and constantly trying to sit beside you. I (Arlene) believe my youngest daughter, Lucy, age four, has physical touch as her primary love language because she always wants to sit next me and one of her favorite words is *Huggie!* She tells me every day to scratch her back, and the first thing she does in the morning is come in my room for her hug.

When you put your arm around your child, wrestle, or give him a high five, you're communicating your love and interest in being together. Physical touch communicates love in a powerful way to all children, not just young children. Throughout elementary school, middle school, and high school, your child still has a strong need for physical touch. A hug given as he leaves each morning may be the difference between emotional security and insecurity throughout the day. A hug when he returns home may determine whether he has a good evening or makes a rambunctious effort to get your attention. Older boys tend to be responsive to more vigorous contact such as wrestling, playful hitting, bear hugs, high fives, and the like. Girls like this type of physical touch also, but they like the softer touches of hugs and holding hands. Screens can't do any of these things, no matter how advanced they are.

love language #2: words of affirmation

Long before they can understand the meaning of words, children receive emotional messages. The tone of voice, the gentleness of mood, and the sense of caring communicate emotional warmth and love. Young children grow in their ability to use words and concepts, guided by the words of their parents. Frequent words of love, instruction, and encouragement are essential to a healthy child—especially if her primary love language is words of affirmation.

Yet with the rise of screen time, many children are hearing more words from their screens than from actual conversation with family members. A child isn't going to get meaningful words of affirmation from a television or tablet. Even if he wins a video game and sees the screen flash, that can't be equated with hearing someone who loves him say, "Well done!"

There's very little a device can do to provide words of affirmation unless a parent uses the device to speak or text words of affirmation to his or her child. Maybe when your older child is walking home from school, you can text, "I'm thinking of how pretty you looked when you went to school today. See you soon." Technology can play a role in delivering positive words to your child, but obviously your affirming words shouldn't be limited to that.

Kids whose love language is words of affirmation need a steady stream of words of affection, praise, and encouragement that communicate, "I care about you." Encouraging words are most effective when they are focused on a specific effort. The goal is to catch your child doing something good and then commend him for it. "I saw how you shared your toys with Christian. I like that. You did a great job being a friend."

Children also need affirming words of guidance. "That's right. That's how to spell your name." "Don't give up; I believe you can do it!" All children are being guided by someone or something. If you as the parent are not their primary guide, then other influences assume that role—with screen time leading the way. Ask yourself this question if you're concerned about your child's screen time use: "Is my child receiving positive and loving guidance from their screen time?"

If not, you may want to reconsider screen time use in your home. When a child's primary love language is words of affirmation, nothing is more important to her sense of being loved than to hear a parent verbally affirm her. Sometimes a preoccupation with screens on the part of the parent or child can stop that flow of positive words to a child's heart.

love language #3: quality time

Six-year-old Nathan taps on his mother's arm. "Mommy, will you play a game with me?"

"I can't play right now," Jean says. "I have to finish answering my emails. Maybe later, okay?"

In ten minutes, Nathan is back and wondering if his mom is finished with her emails. "No, I'm not done yet. Please stop bugging me. I'll let you know when I'm finished."

Nathan sat down on the sofa. He flipped on the television and began searching for a program he liked. Jean noticed the TV was on, and although she wasn't crazy about Nathan watching too much TV, she was relieved to have him out of her hair for a little bit.

When Nathan's program ended, Jean cringed. She knew Nathan would be coming in any second to ask if she was ready to play. And sure enough, he did. "Why don't you watch just one more program?" she said. If she had another thirty minutes, she could finish her to-do list and then give her attention to Nathan.

The chances are good that Nathan was revealing his primary love language—quality time. What really makes him feel loved is his mother's undivided attention. This was so important to him that he returned to his mom again and again. If Jean had played with Nathan for fifteen minutes, she probably would have gotten her work done in peace later in the evening.

In many homes, children would miss their computers and other electronic devices more than they would miss their father or mother. That's because the bulk of their time is spent playing video games, watching television, or texting friends. Children are more and more influenced by forces outside the family, yet they need the strengthening influence of personal time with their parents.

It's difficult to have quality time with a child when screens are present. Yes, you can talk, text, or email when you are away from each other. You can sit down and enjoy a family movie night. But quality time means your child has your undivided attention, and when a television, phone, or video game is present, he doesn't have that.

Quality time should include loving eye contact. Looking into your child's eyes with care is a powerful way to convey love from your heart to the heart of your child. Unfortunately, between staring at computers during school and work and regularly gazing at devices, parents and children have less time left over for looking into each other's eyes.

When Jean takes time to play with her son, it's not only about *doing* things together. Quality time is a means for *knowing* your child better. As you spend time with your children, you will find that a natural result often is good conversation about everything related to your lives.

love language #4: gifts

You might think that every child has the primary love language of gifts, judging from the way they beg for things. It's true that all children want to have more and more, but those whose language of love is receiving gifts will respond differently when they get a gift. They will always make much of receiving the gift. They will want the present to be wrapped or at least given in a unique and creative way. Often they will ooh and aah as they open the gift. It will seem like a big deal to them—and it is. They want your undivided attention as they open the gift. Once they have opened the gift, they will hug you or thank you profusely.

The gift will be placed in a prominent place, and they will show it to you again and again in the next few days. The gift holds a special place in their hearts because it is in fact an expression of your love. It doesn't matter if the gift was made, found, or bought; it matters because you thought of that child.

The digital age has put gift-giving on steroids. Thousands of commercials and advertisements parade the latest toys and gadgets, creating desires in children that did not exist thirty seconds before. Parents and grandparents may choose to shower children with so many presents that the kids' rooms look like disorganized toy stores. With such excess, the gifts lose their specialness. Many children have more toys than they can possibly experience. Lavishing too many gifts is like taking a child into the toy department and saying, "All of this belongs to you." The child may be excited at first, but after a while he'll find himself running in all directions and actually playing with nothing.

Parents and grandparents may need to give less rather than more, carefully choosing meaningful gifts. The following questions can help you evaluate whether or not to purchase a toy or electronic device for your child:

- What message does this toy or device communicate to my child?
- Is it a message with which I am comfortable?
- What might my child learn from playing with this toy or device?
- Will its overall effect be positive or negative?
- Is this a toy or device we can afford?

Not every toy needs to be educational, but they should all serve some positive purpose in the life of your children. Beware of buying electronic devices that expose your children to value systems far removed from those of your family. They already get much of this on television, from neighbors, and from friends at school.

Don't allow advertising or popular culture to convince you that you have to buy expensive gifts like the latest tablets and smartphones for your child. In this wired world, gifts for kids are a lot more expensive than they were years ago. If you opt to give your child a tablet, phone, or other electronic device, it should be given as a gesture of your love. Make a special effort to wrap the gift beautifully and make it a big event. As you give the gift, say something like, "I love you. I feel like you are of the age where this will be beneficial to you. I'll help you understand the responsibilities involved." Make the most of the gift emotionally to communicate your love to your child.

A little girl named Elizabeth, six, reminds us that gifts come in all sorts of shapes and sizes. "Have you ever met the love man? He is right over there," she said, pointing to an older gentleman. "He gives all the children gum." Isn't it nice that it doesn't take a lot of money to show a child love?

love language #5: acts of service

If service is your child's primary love language, your acts of service will communicate most deeply that you love him or her. When you fix a bicycle chain, mend a dress, pack a lunch, or help with homework, your child's love tank fills up. She feels that you love her. This does not mean you must jump at every request. But it does mean you should be sensitive to your child's requests and recognize that your service means a great deal to your child.

You may wonder how your children will develop their own independence and competence if you serve them. Keep in mind that acts of service should be age-appropriate. You don't spoon-feed a five-year-old or make the bed of an eight-year-old because acts of service is his primary love language. As children grow older, we teach them to serve themselves and then others. They will eventually learn how to set the table, wash dishes, vacuum the floor, and clean their rooms.

These are skills children cannot learn online. It's hard to serve others and allow others to serve you if you are constantly digitally connected. A parent could help a child on the computer or show a child how to charge up the battery on a device, but other than that, the opportunities to share acts of service are limited with screens.

On my (Arlene's) shelf, there sits a small skunk—a stuffed animal with a hole that needs to be sewn. I'm not a seamstress, so that may explain why it's been there more than two weeks. Frankly, I feel too busy to get to that skunk between writing, blogging, emails, Facebook, Twitter, etc. Although technology is supposed to serve us, many times we find ourselves serving it, with little time left over in the day for acts of service like sewing up stuffed skunks for little girls.

Perhaps you have experienced this in your home. Acts of service have been sacrificed for screen time. Instead of responding to your child's request to help put up a poster in his room or find a set of lost markers, you're on the computer. "I'm sorry, honey, I can't do that now. I'll do it later, okay?" After receiving this kind of response day after day, your child may question your love for him.

No doubt parenting is a service-oriented vocation from the moment your crying baby enters the world. Because service to a child is constant for so many years, parents can forget that the daily and mundane acts they perform are actually expressions of love with long-term effects. Many times parents feel more like slaves than loving servants. However, if they assume this attitude, it will communicate itself emotionally to the child, who will feel that he is receiving little love from the acts of service. His physical needs may be met, but his emotional development will be greatly hampered. Even the best parents need to stop for an attitude check now and then, to be sure that their acts of service are communicating love.

Your children need to experience your caring acts of service so they can be taught by example to show concern for others. In the Chapman family, we had an open house every Friday night for college students during the early '70s. We'd pack in twenty to sixty students. The format was simple. From 8:00 to 10:00 p.m. we had a discussion about a relational, moral, or social issue, drawn from a Bible passage. Next came refreshments and informal conversation. At midnight we kicked them out.

Our children, Shelley and Derek, were young during those years and wandered in and out of the meetings. It wasn't unusual to find one of them sleeping in a student's lap by the fireplace or talking with someone. The students were our extended family, and the children looked forward to Friday evenings. Often on Saturday mornings, some of the students would return for "Do-Good Projects" like raking leaves for the elderly or other jobs that needed to get done. Shelley and Derek always went along on these service projects, even though they jumped in the leaves more than they raked them.

Sharing our home with others and involving the children at a young age in service had a profound and positive effect in their lives. Make it your goal that your children will learn to be comfortable in serving others. Your children will not pick this up by accident or online. Rather, they will learn it by watching you serve them and other people with joy.

Now that you have been introduced to the five love languages, you may be wondering, *What's my child's primary love language?* You might want to read *The 5 Love Languages of Children,* or visit www.5LoveLanguages.com to play The Love Languages Mystery Game.

There are some children who don't feel loved by their parents, not because the parents don't love them but because they are not getting enough

5 Ways to Trade Screen Time for Serve Time

1. Help your child practice for her sports team, such as pitching and catching for baseball or shooting free throws for basketball.

2. Wake up half an hour earlier to make a special surprise breakfast for your children.

3. Make a list of your child's favorite screen-free things to do with you. Then periodically do one of his favorites when the child least expects it.

4. Create flash cards for your child's upcoming test or quiz. Work together until he feels confident with the material.

5. Assist your child in fixing a favorite broken toy or bicycle. Simply taking the time to repair it communicates love to a child whose love language is acts of service.

love in their specific love language. These children tend to be lethargic and more apt to withdraw from people. In today's world, the natural place to withdraw is into screen time with a tablet, television, game console, or phone. The technology itself isn't to blame; the screen is simply the modern withdrawing place for a child when he doesn't feel loved by his parents.

Many parents welcome screens into their home because they don't want their children to fall behind technologically. But these parents may not be aware that a child can fall behind *emotionally*, with much more significant personal drawbacks. A child can fall behind to the extent that he or she can never catch up.

As you learn to consistently speak the languages of love to your child—physical touch, words of affirmation, quality time, receiving gifts, and acts of service—you are giving your child the intellectual and emotional stimulation he desperately needs in order to thrive. What you do in loving your child will show the world that the language of love isn't most powerfully spoken in pixels or posts but by parents.

> *"The Fear-of-God builds up confidence,*
> *and makes a world safe for your children."*
> —PROVERBS 14:26 *THE MESSAGE*

chapter eleven

screen time and
security

Amy and Bill tried their best to create a safe online environment for their ten-year-old daughter, Kendra. Screen time was limited to two hours per day, and no electronic devices were allowed in her bedroom. Kendra used the computer or cellphone in a common area like the kitchen table or family room. With Internet filters installed on the computer and phones, Kendra's parents felt secure about her screen time.

What they didn't realize was Kendra's growing affection for a popular social networking site for kids. She logged in every day to play games, chat with screen friends, and read the fashion blog. Although the website was marketed as safe for kids, she was watching trailers for PG-13 movies and in the chat room reading responses to "How do I know if he likes me?" Kendra became more self-conscious about her appearance and started worrying because no boys at school seemed to like her. She was being influenced by the comments she read online from other kids, and her parents didn't know anything about it.

Kendra uses a social networking site geared for kids ages nine to sixteen, and as you can imagine, there's a big difference developmentally between those ages. What may be appropriate for a sixteen-year-old is not healthy for ten-year-old Kendra.

Rules about screen use are certainly helpful and necessary, but there is something more valuable for your child's security. It involves active participation as a parent in screen-time education and use, along with your commitment to shape your child's character.

the bully-proof heart

When many parents think about Internet security, they focus on pedophiles, stranger danger, and other cyber-horror stories. Perhaps that's because the tragedies force us to pay attention to our children's digital use. Like the story of a twelve-year-old girl who jumped to her death from an abandoned cement factory tower. Two girls, ages twelve and fourteen, were arrested on felony charges for allegedly taunting and bullying her, posting things like "Drink bleach and die."[1]

Stories like this are heartbreaking and serve as a wake-up call to take cyberbullying seriously. Parents must make children aware of stranger danger, but it's more likely that the damage done to a child online will come from someone she knows. Cyberbullying is using digital media intentionally to communicate false, hostile, or embarrassing information about another person. It's the most common online risk for tweens and teens. It can happen to any young person online and can cause serious outcomes such as depression, anxiety, and severe isolation.

According to one national survey of fourth to eighth graders:

- 42 percent have been bullied while online (one in four had it happen more than once).

- 35 percent have been threatened online (nearly one in five had it happen more than once).
- 21 percent have received mean or threatening email or other messages.
- 53 percent admit having said something mean or hurtful to another person online.
- 58 percent have not told their parents or an adult about something hurtful that happened online.[2]

According to Parry Aftab, executive director of WiredSafety.org, cyberbullying is beginning in second grade as kids use text messaging and interactive websites much earlier. "It starts at six or seven these days. It generally tends to fall off at about the age of fourteen. After that, you may have cyberstalking and harassment, but it tends to be more sexually oriented; you break up with a girl or boy, you target them because you're unhappy."[3]

Kids making fun of one another and saying hateful words is nothing new. But technology can magnify and spread a hurtful comment to damage and frighten a child like never before. Young children are not emotionally equipped to handle digital hits to their self-esteem. Kids are posting each other's secrets, stealing passwords, and attacking others while posing as someone else, and taking inappropriate pictures to share online to embarrass.

As parents, we are responsible to foster the mental and emotional health of our children. We cannot throw up our hands and say, "I just don't understand the latest technology." That's like allowing a child to run unsupervised in a crowded mall because we can't decipher the store directory. We must become familiar and comfortable on digital turf so we can guide our children safely and well-informed through the modern digital playground.

Every child needs to develop relational skills so that she will treat all persons as having equal value and will be able to build healthy, positive friendships face to face and online. A child lacking essential relational skills might become a controlling bully who lacks empathy and treats others cruelly. Or she may become a victim of bullying who doesn't know how to ask for help. You can help your child develop a bully-proof heart by incorporating these guidelines:

- Your child should report any cyberbullying incidents to you (Mom and Dad).
- Your child should block bullies and not ever respond to their comments.
- Talk with your child about the dangers of attacking others online.
- Teach your child never to post anything she wouldn't be comfortable showing you or her teacher.
- If your child receives a hurtful comment, tell him five things you like about him.
- Actively supervise your child's time online.

If your child is the one doing the bullying, let him know you are not going to condemn him. He may feel guilty about what he has done and never express his feelings again, especially if he is responsive to authority. Part of training is to let him know that you accept him as a person and always want to know how he is feeling, whether happy or sad or angry. From that place of unconditional love, you can work with him to correct his behavior in the future.

predators, privacy, and porn

In 1996, the Justice Department's cyber crimes section opened 113 cases for the sexual exploitation of children committed over the Internet. Through the fiscal year 2007, that number grew to 20,200 cases.[4] This terrible crime against children has grown exponentially over the years. As a parent, it's wise to learn about the behavior of sexual predators so you can know what you and your children should avoid online. Chat rooms for kids are not only problematic because of cyberbullying, but they are also a nesting place for predators. Explain to your child that people in chat rooms may not be who they seem to be. Someone who says she is a thirteen-year-old girl may actually be a forty-year-old man. Just because it's written online doesn't make it true.

According to FBI special agent Peter Brust, it's common for sexual predators to compile buddy lists on multiple hard drives and computers. They may have more than a thousand buddies lined up and catalogued. They know what time they're on at night and what they like. "I'm surprised at the number of times I go to give school presentations or parent group presentations when the parents say, 'I had no idea that my child was a member of this social networking site or had this screen name or profile,'" said Brust.[5]

In this agent's interviews with teen victims and non-victims, the non-victims have something in common: they are savvy about the safety issues of the Internet and value their privacy. On the other hand, teen victims are usually looking for information about sex; they are looking for romance and connection. Predators play into this. Through many online conversations they build enough trust to actually meet the teen.

on privacy

Websites and mobile apps collect significant amounts of personal information from children. When kids are asked to register with a site in order to play a game, read a blog post, or enter a contest, they may be asked to input their name, street address or city, birthday, and favorite activities or commercial products. This information can be used to create customer lists that are sold to businesses.

Teach your older children to read the privacy policy statements on the websites and mobile apps they are visiting. Learn what information is collected and what it is used for. You can also look for a web privacy "seal of approval" on the first page. To display a legitimate logo, participants must agree to post their privacy policies and submit to audits of their privacy practices.

Social networking sites like Facebook and Instagram require a child to be thirteen years old to sign up. The Children's Online Privacy Protection Act (COPPA) restricts websites from getting personal data about minors. However, as you may know from your own experience or from friends, many children lie about their age, with some 7.5 million minors allegedly signing on.[6]

If your ten-year-old wants to be on Facebook with her classmates and Grandma, what's the harm? Should this be a concern to you as a parent? First of all, there is the issue of lying about one's age. If you are going to assist your child, what does that communicate about telling the truth? If your child does it without your permission, that undermines your authority. Then there is the matter of strangers seeing your child's profile. When your child turns eighteen and becomes an adult according to her records on Facebook (when in reality she may only be fifteen), strangers could also see her and a list of her friends.

On Instagram, by default, anyone can see the photos that you upload unless you set your profile to private (that way only the people on your friend and follower list can see your photos). When uploading a photo, the geo-location of the photo can be easily shared, so you want to be sure your children always have geotagging off.

Snapchat is an app that allows users to take a photo and share it with someone for up to ten seconds before it disappears and is permanently deleted. This app is marketed for teenagers and is a perfect vehicle for sexting. *Sexting* is the increasingly common practice of sending sexually suggestive text messages, photos, or videos. Although the Snapchat photo disappears, the recipient may take a screen shot of the photo, or a picture of the photo. If your child sends an inappropriate photo because she thinks it will disappear in ten seconds, she may suffer harm when that photo is stored and then perhaps shared with others.

In this digital age, privacy must be vigilantly guarded by parents. Many children and tweens do not yet possess the wisdom to understand the value of privacy.

on porn

Pornography is easier to find than ever. The days of going to a seedy part of town to browse an adult bookstore are long over. Porn is available on scores of devices that we use every day—phones, computers, and tablets. Consider these sobering statistics:

- 12 percent of websites on the Internet are pornographic.
- One in three porn viewers are women.
- 70 percent of men aged 18–24 visit porn sites in a typical month.
- 34 percent of Internet users have experienced unwanted exposure to porn through pop-up ads, misdirected links, or emails.
- The average age a child sees porn online is eleven.[7]

A child could simply be curious or may accidentally click on a link while doing a Google search. Even with a good computer filter, children can find ways to access porn, like through Peer-to-Peer Networking (P2P), an application that runs on your computer and allows you to share files with other P2P users. Once you have a peer-to-peer application installed, you can allow anyone in the world to copy files from your home PC. Thirty-five percent of peer-to-peer downloads are pornographic in nature. When children stumble upon porn on the Internet, they typically find still photos. Hard-core pornography is unavailable without being purchased with a credit card. But with peer-to-peer sharing, children can view a free triple-X-rated movie that may not be blocked by the Internet filter. To prevent this from happening, check your computers periodically to make sure no one has downloaded any P2P file-sharing networks such as BitTorrent, Bearshare, or Limewire.

Although viewing porn once probably isn't going to have long-term effects on your child, viewing it on a regular basis will. The more graphic the porn, the more destructive it is to the mind and heart of your child. Pornography misinforms children and confuses them about human sexuality. There is the devaluing of women, the exaltation of "perfect" body types, and the creation of false expectations that will be carried into a future relationship. Kids view porn secretly, which is dishonoring to their parents while causing shame in the heart of the child.

Before a child stumbles upon pornographic material, it's imperative for parents to be open with their children about sexuality. Explain to your child differences between males and females. Using appropriate drawings, show what a male body looks like and what a female body looks like. Have an honest talk about what is going to happen to your child's body when he or she becomes a teenager. Explaining these things long before they happen helps your child understand that sexuality is not a taboo topic.

Talk with your child about Adam and Eve and how God clothed them for a reason. Then you can talk about pornography and how it violates that decency. Explain that someday pictures of naked people or partially naked people will pop up on the screen. When that happens, instruct your child to close that window right away and come and tell you about it.

We suggest having several short conversations about sexuality and porn, so it's not just one long, marathon talk with your child wondering, "When will this be over?" Remember to bring up this topic more frequently as your children become tweens and teens. Your children need and want your guidance to understand how their bodies work and how to navigate their sexual feelings.

Set family guidelines about pornography. Let your children know what the consequences will be if you find out they are viewing pornography. Enforce boundaries while keeping your tone calm and your heart soft toward your child. Admitting to pornography use is embarrassing, and if a child feels that his parent will shame him, he may work hard to keep his pornography use a secret.

If you discover your child is viewing pornography regularly and cannot seem to stop, seek a professional counselor who can direct your child away from this unhealthy behavior. Do not allow your son or daughter to be brought up with pornography. Its negative effects could impact your child into adulthood.

home safe home

Even with the pitfalls of the Internet, technology has its upsides. Seven-year-old Ava had a big smile on her face when her mom picked her up from school. She had a Skype date with Daddy after dinner that night. Ava's father was deployed with the military for six months, and the Skype dates really helped to keep the family connected. A few weeks earlier, when Ava was having trouble with her math homework, her dad had helped her solve a problem even though he was thousands of miles away.

"Hi, Dad!" Ava said loudly as her arms waved back and forth across the screen. "Look!" she exclaimed, pulling her lips apart with her fingers. "I lost a tooth!"

"Wow," Ava's dad replied laughing. "Look at my teeth. I still have them all and haven't lost a one!"

Years ago, it would have been impossible for Ava's dad to talk with her in real time and see the gap where her tooth once was. Now video calling makes it possible for families to stay in touch when they are geographically separated. That connection with loved ones through technology can make a child feel secure and loved.

In your home, how can you use technology to foster a feeling of security for your child? As you think about creating a "Home Safe Home" with screens, you can ask some clarifying questions about your family's media use:

- Do we use screens to come together as a family? If so, how?

- Are parent/child relationships primarily strengthened or weakened because of screen use?

- Is screen time at home promoting learning and positive values?

- Are my children learning bad words or attitudes after being exposed to something on screens?

Your home should be a place of security for your child, a warm and loving environment. Home isn't meant to be a place where individual family members retreat to their screens to become engrossed in the news of politics or the playground. In today's digital world, you must think about the role screens will play in your home. Perhaps it's unrealistic to have a screen-free home, but what about a screen-smart and screen-safe home?

One good rule of thumb is to keep all electronic media out of the children's room, particularly with younger children. You don't know what goes on after the door is closed and the lights go out. Watching screens before bedtime in a child's room can interrupt healthy sleep patterns, not to mention give a child unsupervised access to objectionable content.

Yet the reality is that many children today have a television or computer in their room. Seventy-one percent of eight- to eighteen-year-olds have a TV in their bedroom.[8] One reason is convenience. If the adults in the home want to watch one program and the kids want to watch another, why not let the kids watch in a different room? It's no longer necessary to take turns and make sacrifices for one another. Advances in technology allow all of us to get what we want when we want it. Individual preferences, both for parents and children, become paramount.

We may be gaining the convenience of multiple screens, but we are losing out on opportunities to bond like the family of yesteryear who gathered around the television to watch the same program. It's the togetherness we long for, not the nostalgia of a different era. There's no going back to the black-and-white television of the 1950s—and most of us are grateful for that. Technology gives our children access to all sorts of information, both good and bad. It's up to us as parents to guide our children to the positives of technology, while minimizing risks.

The family computer or tablet should be used in an open location everyone can see. Many families collect all electronic devices at night, placing cellphones, tablets, and gaming devices in a bin stored in the parents' bedroom overnight. Nighttime is a logical time not to have access to phones and other screens. There may be exceptions to this; for instance, if there's been a lot of crime in the neighborhood, you might want your child to have a phone near his bed.

Besides keeping tabs on *where* the electronics are in your home, you can practice Internet safety by filtering *what* can be viewed. Internet safety software can protect your family from harmful content by blocking questionable websites, videos, music, instant messages, and social networks. Some systems let parents pick among predetermined categories; others provide a list that allows parents to add or remove sites. A blacklist filters out websites based on categories like sexually explicit material or graphic violence. Filters do this generally by searching the web address, keywords in the site, and keyword searches. You also use a "white list" by generating a list of approved websites that are the only ones your child can search while online.

Installing filters on your computers and phones is a recommended practice, but, of course, it does not guarantee that your child will not see something inappropriate. Some kids will stumble upon something too sexual or violent; other kids will seek it out. A child who is determined to view something off-limits can find a way around filters and monitoring systems.

You don't want to have a false sense of security simply because you have a first-rate Internet safety system in place. Instead of relying on technology to safeguard your child's Internet use, take action as a parent to supervise your child and constantly give instruction about digital safety. Eventually, the best filter for a growing child is his own eyes and ears, as his parents teach him what is healthy and unhealthy online and on screens.

but everyone else has a cellphone

Many fifth and sixth graders at my (Arlene's) kids' school have a cellphone just like mine. You probably know children that young or younger who have their own phones. So how young is too young for a cellphone? Every child and family circumstance is different, so there is no magic age to answer that question. However, children in elementary school do not need access to the Internet on their phones. Giving a child the responsibility of browsing the Internet safely is an unreasonable expectation. It's like letting a child loose alone in a mall with adult bookstores and drug dealers, hoping she will stay out of trouble.

If you are going to give a child a cellphone, pick a basic phone with no photo sending abilities or Internet access. Make sure the phone is used for safety reasons, and monitor how your child is using it. You can put a specific amount of minutes on the phone and have it shut down between certain hours at night. Parents should also show their child the monthly bill so a child understands that cellphone service is not free. They can begin to learn financial responsibility and an appreciation for the devices Mom and Dad provide.

For the first month of cellphone use, you might consider having your child use the phone exclusively to call Mom or Dad. In the second month, expand that to calling one or two trusted friends. When parents provide freedom gradually, it can help them monitor how a child is handling those freedoms. You can create a cellphone contract from the start so expectations of use are clearly communicated and there are no surprises. Your contract may include the following:

- I will not give my cellphone number to anyone unless I clear it with my parents.

- I will not take my phone into the classroom if it is prohibited.

- I will always answer calls from my parents. If I am in class, I will call them back as soon as I can.

- I will pay for any charges above and beyond the usual monthly fee.

Jackson and his friend Connor, both age eleven, have been friends since kindergarten. They've grown up going to each other's homes to play. Recently, Connor got a cellphone with Internet access. Connor and Jackson would take turns using the phone to play video games at Connor's house. Jackson's mom was concerned about her son having access to the Internet so easily. Yet she knew it was impossible to supervise the boys all the time.

What can you do to keep your child safe when he is on a playdate with someone else? You cannot impose your screen and cellphone rules on another family. Here are a few guidelines for decisions about screen times and friends:

Differentiate the big things from the small things. Ask yourself, "Will this matter a week from now?" If your child is viewing porn at someone's house, the answer will be yes. But if he is playing thirty minutes of nonviolent video games, the answer is probably no. It's like eating junk food at someone's house; as long as your son eats healthy foods at home, a candy bar at a friend's house isn't going to harm him.

Get to know the other family. Take the time to befriend the parents of your children's friends. You need to be able to ask, "What types of television shows and video games do you allow in your home? Do you monitor what the boys are watching?" Don't think it is rude to ask; it is your responsibility to create safe boundaries for your child even when he is away from you.

Make yourself the fall guy. You might fear appearing judgmental and superior if you ask too many questions. Just tell the other parent you are overprotective. It's more gracious to criticize yourself ("Forgive me if I'm such a

163

high-maintenance parent") than to implicate the more lenient parent.

If you find your family's screen-time values are not compatible with the other family's, it's probably a good idea to have your son distance himself from that friend after school. Every family has the right to have different values. It's not a case of your son being too good for another boy. It's a matter of you being the protector of your child. It is your responsibility to filter what goes into your child's heart and mind through her eyes and ears. There is no Internet-safety substitute for an involved parent.

Screen-Safe Family Pledge

Start with the following pledge and modify it to fit your family's needs:

- *I will never give out personal information such as my last name, address, or phone number.*
- *I will not give out the name of my school, city, or parent's workplace.*
- *I will not share my passwords with anyone.*
- *I will follow the time limits my family sets.*
- *I will allow my parents to check into my media history whenever they think it is necessary.*
- *I will only have online interactions with people I know in real life.*
- *I will tell my mom or dad right away if anything I see makes me uncomfortable or if anyone asks to meet me.*
- *I will not stay on or click on a page that says, "For Over 18 Years Only."*
- *I will not download any pictures or files unless a parent is supervising me.*
- *I will not send pictures of myself or my family to anyone online without my parent's permission.*
- *I will not say anything online that I wouldn't say in person.*

"Rules without relationship lead to rebellion."

—JOSH MCDOWELL

screen time and
parental authority

My (Arlene's) husband, James, was at the park when he saw a dad with his two kids riding bicycles down the street without helmets. They were similar in age to our kids, about five and seven at the time. The kids stopped to play in the playground, so James struck up a conversation with the dad, asking, "Why don't your kids wear bicycle helmets?"

"I can't get my kids to wear them," he replied with a sigh. "They refuse to ride their bikes if they have to put on helmets."

James was dumbfounded. We are huge fans of bicycle safety for a very personal reason. When our son, Ethan, was riding his bike home from school in second grade, he didn't stop at a neighborhood stop sign. As he made a wide right turn, he hit an oncoming car. That was probably the scariest moment of James's life as he turned that same corner on his bike to see Ethan lying in the road. The ambulance came to take Ethan to Children's Hospital. His bike was ruined; his helmet was dented, but Ethan emerged that evening from the hospital with only a few bruises.

The outcome of that accident would have been tragic if Ethan had not been wearing a helmet. James shared this story with that dad in the park, hoping it would motivate him to make his children wear bike helmets. Sadly he saw them a few weeks later in the park, riding bikes—without helmets.

What would stop a parent from forcing their child to do something essential to that child's safety? Unfortunately, we live in a parenting culture where it is increasingly common for children to call the shots instead of the parents. Somehow adults have given in to little girls in pigtails and angry, young boys who aren't getting their way. Yet *parents* are responsible for the rearing of children, not the other way around. Adults are older and wiser. We know what a child needs to understand in our culture by the time he reaches eighteen. It's our job to deliver our children into adulthood with everything they need to thrive.

Parenting is not a place where you can pass the buck. The responsibility for raising your child isn't shouldered by the school, government, religious organization, or child-care worker. Although the involvement of community is important, your child needs you to be his primary teacher at every stage of his life.

Legendary comic and actor Bill Cosby was interviewed about his television program *The Cosby Show*. Drawn from his own life experience, the hit sitcom portrayed strong parenting and role modeling that has become virtually nonexistent in present day television. "I based the series on two important things," said Cosby. "Number one . . . I hated those series where the children were brighter than the parents, and those parents had to play dumb. Number two was that I wanted to take the house back."[1]

Do you need to "take your house back"? Contemporary parenting has catered to many a child's whim and become something of a popularity contest. We long to be liked by our kids and fear rocking the boat with them relationally. Or we simply don't have the wherewithal to deal with tantrums, tears, and other battles of the will. It's important to remind yourself that you are the parent, not the friend, of your child. Of course, you want to act friendly and speak in your child's love languages, but you must also be the authority figure. Your child will have dozens and dozens of friends as she grows up, but she will only ever have one mother and one father.

Rod, father of two daughters ages seven and nine, walked into his living room. His girls were curled up on the couch; one was texting on a phone, and the other was playing a video game. The TV was turned on to a sitcom geared for preteens. Neither girl seemed to be watching, so Rod switched the channel to ESPN. The girls both looked up and protested, "Hey, we were watching that!"

Later, Rod posted this comment on Facebook: "My kids seem to think that if they are sitting in front of the TV, they have rights to the TV even if they are not watching. In my world, they are not really watching TV. They are on their computer and phone. Am I wrong here?"

Rod may be taking an informal parenting poll, but regardless of popular opinion, parents should have the authority to decide what is being watched and by whom. But without clear leadership, today's child feels entitled to choose whatever pleases him or her.

a different world

Parents are needed more than ever to provide instruction, correction, and positive modeling to a child regarding screen time, even if this digital world seems like unfamiliar territory. We live in a brand-new era when children are digital natives and many parents are digital immigrants. In other words, many children know more about technology than their parents, and that is quite different from how the world worked hundreds of years ago.

During the print age, parents could read and have access to information that children could not. This led to an elevated status for adults and a clear delineation of childhood. Broadcast media then allowed children to peek into the world of adults through television, a world formerly hidden in books children couldn't read.

Now the positions have almost flip-flopped. Parents struggle to understand the wired lives of children and teens, asking their children for advice on everything from passwords to texting. Apps can teach your child how to multiply or to speak a foreign language. It's easy for parents to step back and let the phone become a child's tutor. Children may have more digital sense than their parents, but they still need the common sense of an authority figure to guide them.

If you have a tablet, maybe you've wondered, "Is this my tablet or my child's? She uses it more than I do!" Kids have become the beneficiaries of their parents' costly electronic devices. The lines between children and adults are becoming blurred. We are using the same devices with access to the same benefits and dangers of the Internet. With texting, children have social lives online like their parents do. Sometimes kids are more immersed in technology than their parents.

Don't give up your influence as a parent just because you don't understand the latest gadget or website. Learn what apps and websites your children are using. Ask other parents to help you or take courses to gain a basic understanding. You cannot be left behind while your child journeys alone to a rapidly evolving world of screens. Without parental authority, Google becomes the answer to life's questions.

evaluate your family's digital life

We live not only in a multicultural world; we live in a multi-moral generation. People have all sorts of different ideas about what is right or wrong. Many moral standards that have been embraced for centuries are being questioned. On-screen entertainment often goes against the morals we are trying to instill in our children. But we are not responsible for what others do or create; we are responsible for our family. Parents have the freedom and the right to decide what they will allow their children to watch.

If you've ever watched the Super Bowl with young children by your side, you've probably been appalled by the sexuality in the commercials and music at halftime. Unfortunately, this type of MTV-style programming is what many teenagers watch today. If we're not careful, our children will be exposed to adult content and vulgarity way too early. As a parent, make it your business to evaluate everything your kids bring into the home. What music do they listen to? What are they watching on television or on DVD?

You can prevent moral decay in your child by helping him make wise media choices. After you watch it, talk about a program and what values it promotes. Learn the lyrics of your kids' favorite songs and make sure they are clean. Eventually, as your child grows into a teenager, you will spend more time listening to your child's opinion and discussing media choices together. But while your child is elementary school-aged or younger, you can set and enforce standards of what is acceptable and not acceptable.

Sometimes you have to go against the grain to protect your family's values. When you don't allow your child to watch a movie other kids are watching, it doesn't mean you think those families are bad people. It just means that, in your judgment, that movie is not good for your child. In the same way you give another family the freedom to decide what is best for their kids, accept that freedom for yourself without any guilt. Don't cave in to peer pressure or make decisions in order not to offend anyone. Instead evaluate your child's screen time with these easy ABCs:

Attitude: What is my child's attitude like after the screen time?
Behavior: How does the content encourage my child to behave?
Character: What character traits are being modeled and picked up?

Take a moment right now to evaluate your child's current digital habits.

How is screen time affecting your child's attitude? His behavior? His character? Are you pleased with the content and amount of screen time your child has each day?

Brooke is a mother of two daughters, ages eleven and thirteen. She and her husband don't have stated screen-time rules, but they try to have the kids watch age-appropriate programs. The girls usually watch about three hours of TV on school days and up to six hours on a Saturday or Sunday.

"I am concerned about the amount of time the girls are spending in front of a screen," Brooke said. "I feel it has made them more mouthy and reluctant to go on family outings. We tried to change the family rules, and they didn't like that. We became lazy about enforcing it."

Brooke and her husband are unhappy about the influence of media on the girls' attitude and behavior, yet they are not willing to make unpopular changes. Remind yourself that parenting has little to do with being popular. Instead, it requires backbone and thick skin to make changes in the screen-time rules whenever necessary.

creating digital-free zones

It's Saturday, and you know it's an ideal day to ride bikes together or visit that new museum the kids have been talking about. But the day gets off to a slow start. The kids flip on the TV after breakfast, and you end up watching a movie. After three hours of watching television, you feel lethargic and it seems like way too much work to get everyone out the door.

What happened to your Saturday? Your plans for a great day out got hijacked by the convenience of staying in. The remote control was just seconds away, but the new museum was a whole twenty miles away. Screens—the phone, computer, tablet, or TV—have become a default activity for many families. It requires no extra effort and becomes as habitual as brushing one's teeth in the morning. Willpower alone will not change your family's screen-time use. You must create new habits and rewire your child's brain to enjoy screen-free activities.

Perhaps you have heard that environment is stronger than willpower. That's true when it comes to eating (it's hard to maintain willpower in a bakery), and it's also true when it comes to screen time. If you instruct your child to limit her screen time to two hours a day but give her a television in her bedroom and a tablet loaded with her favorite games, she is going to struggle. It's like trying to resist eating sweets with a big plate of freshly baked cookies sitting on the table in front of you. That tempting environment would quickly drain a person's self-control, regardless of willpower.

Help your child practice self-control with screens by literally creating digital-free zones at home. If your child has instant, easy access to screens 24/7, he will be constantly pulled to use them. Many parents give a child a personal phone way too early. It's incredibly difficult to self-regulate screen time when you have a phone in your pocket with you at all times. If you do give your child a cellphone or tablet, set clear limits and regularly check if those limits are being obeyed. To give a child a phone or iPad with no limitations, no boundaries, no instructions, and no expectations is extremely detrimental to a child of any age.

So how do you create pockets of digital-free space for your children at home? Here are a few ideas.

Make your child's bedroom a digital-free zone. Don't place a television in your child's room. Collect all devices such as phones and tablets at nighttime for safekeeping. Set a time, such as 7:30 p.m., to gather up all portable electronics. Be purposeful to do this for one month; after that time period, it will become an automatic habit for the whole family.

Don't allow phones or screens during mealtimes. Family mealtime is a powerful time to connect emotionally with your child. Don't allow digital distractions like answering a text or watching a television show rob your family of this quality time. If your children are in school, they are probably spending more hours a day away from you than with you. With limited time in each day, mealtime with your family becomes even more important.

Preserve car rides for conversation, not for earbuds, movies, or video games. How many times have you seen parents in the front seat of a car and children in the backseat either watching a screen or plugged in with earbuds? That commute is a gift of time alone with your child in a busy world. Don't waste it by letting your children zone out with their devices. Use your drive to talk about the day. Or turn your car into a mobile university by listening to audio books or podcasts together that would be a positive influence and basis for more conversation.

Schedule your child's free time with non-screen activities. Every day a child ought to engage in healthy activities such as playtime, reading time, homework time, conversation time, and physical activity. If your child doesn't participate in a sport, set aside time for outdoor play. If that's not possible in your neighborhood, create an indoor gym with stations for jumping jacks, push-ups, sit-ups, etc. Insist on a daily reading time, and offer your child interesting titles from the library for variety. Encourage playtime by placing board games and toys on shelves your kids can reach. Children develop better if their lives are scheduled and they know what to expect each day. If they can get in the daily routine of reading, doing homework, playing, and exercising, then screen time can be scheduled in to become a *part* of their life, but not the *main* part.

how to change unhealthy patterns

Anna and Tyler were putting off buying a video game console for their boys ages three and five. But with friends and cousins who had video game consoles, the boys were constantly asking for one. To surprise the boys at Christmas, Anna and Tyler decided it was the right time to get the boys their first video game console. Of course, the boys were thrilled. They had established rules—the boys could take turns and each had thirty minutes after breakfast and thirty minutes before dinner. After a few months, however, the boys wanted to play games that seemed too dark for their ages. Anna and Tyler said those games weren't appropriate, but the whining persisted.

Not only were they constantly asking for games geared for older kids, they began asking to use Anna's phone to play games whenever they were out. Even though it was beyond the screen-time limit she had originally set, Anna handed over the phone to the boys at the grocery store to keep them quiet. Then it happened again while waiting at karate practice, then again at the restaurant. Using Anna's phone throughout the day while running errands became normal for the boys. Anna felt terrible about her sons' increased time playing video games. But she didn't know how to take away privileges once they had been given.

I (Gary) counsel many parents like Anna who are afraid to make changes that will upset their children. Your child may throw a temper tantrum, but if you don't deal with that tantrum at age three, he'll still be throwing tantrums at age thirteen. Don't ever let your child's temper tantrum work in his favor. If he gets what he wants by throwing a tantrum, you are training him to throw a tantrum more often because it's effective. Instead tell your child, "If you want to kick your legs and scream, fine. Go do it in your room. But it's not going to make any difference. This is not the way you get things in our house. When you've calmed down, you can tell me what you want. We'll decide if it is something helpful to you. But we never change the rules just because you cry."

Children will resist when you try to change anything and certainly when you restrict patterns of screen time. But as they get involved in other activities, they will eventually come to appreciate what you've done. For instance, if Anna replaces her son's screen time with half an hour of reading time, he might not like that at first. But as he gets into reading wholesome books, which take him into a world of imagination, he is going to come back and thank his mom that she taught him how to make reading a part of his life.

Perhaps you realize you have made some mistakes with giving your child too many privileges or too little supervision of screen time. It's time to have a conversation with your child, perhaps beginning with an apology. Instead of blaming your child for playing too many video games, admit your responsibility. "Mom and I have been thinking about this, and we realize we made a mistake when we gave you this device. You were not old enough for this. So here's what we're going to do: we are going to take away this device for three months. We want you to learn how to live, obey, and enjoy being with people without this device. After three months, we'll see if it would be a good thing for us to give back the device."

By using a time frame such as three months, you don't take away the device indefinitely and make it an endless punishment. You give your child the chance to try something new for a period of time, enough time to break bad habits and establish healthier ones. Maybe you've been letting things slide for quite some time. You had clear guidelines that were violated, and you should have taken action much earlier. You can't change the past, but you can start where you are.

Don't be afraid to make unpopular decisions in the best interest of your child. Your goal as a parent isn't to make your child *feel* good; your goal is to make him *be* a good person. From now on, establish clear boundaries. Communicate the new screen-time rules and what will happen if those rules are broken. Be consistent in applying consequences. Consistency prevents your child from growing resentful because of ever-changing rules.

always for you

Natalie and Brent have four children, ages eighteen, fifteen, thirteen, and ten. The kids get a basic cellphone when they reach high school. They can't send or receive photos or access the Internet on their phones, but they are allowed to use social networking sites like Facebook and Twitter

Screen-Safe Family Pledge
A Note to Grandparents

Nora always used to look forward to her grandchildren's visit. But lately, things have changed. After giving her a hug, her grandkids immediately ask to use her iPad. Once the iPad is out, the kids don't want to play Monopoly with her or sit on the couch to talk. Nora can't compete with the entertainment value of the screen, so she just sits next to the kids while they play games. She misses the old days of being together with her grandkids before she got her iPad.

Have you ever felt like Nora? Try these Do's and Don'ts the next time your grandchild comes for a visit.

DO:

• Make your home a media-free place for your grandkids.

• Center your time together around activities like outdoor walks, playing games, or baking cookies.

• Draw pictures or make crafts together.

• Slow down! Your grandchild's life is probably very busy, and free time with you is priceless.

• Ask your grandchildren questions about school, friends, and life.

• Tell stories of when you were a child and things you have learned and accomplished.

DON'T:

• Feel guilty about disappointing your grandchildren if they don't like the screen-time rules at your house.

• Watch more than two hours a day of television together.

• Give in to their demands for more screen time.

• Allow them to watch or play something they are not allowed to at home.

• Buy your grandchild a device like a cellphone or tablet without clearing it with Mom and Dad first.

at home. Phones and tablets are collected every night, and every Sunday is a "phone-free" day. The two younger kids don't have a phone or email account. They are not allowed to use social media until high school.

Although they have stricter rules than their peers, Natalie and Brent's children have accepted these limits without any major problems. The family rules were clearly articulated to the kids when they were young. There were no surprises like "What do you mean I can't have a cellphone until I'm in high school?" And Natalie and Brent have a strong relationship with their kids. They keep their children's emotional love tanks full by speaking the five love languages. Rules aren't dictated from a stoic parent; they are spoken in love from a caring mom or dad.

Your children need to know you are always for them. There is no computer program in the world comparable to an involved and loving parent providing guidance. When you take your place as the authority figure in the home, your child will become more and more secure in the real world, not the screen world.

> *"The most terrible poverty is loneliness,*
> *and the feeling of being unloved."*
> —MOTHER TERESA

chapter thirteen

screen time and the
single parent

Shana, age ten, sits on the concrete with her backpack next to her. After-school care is over; she sees her mom and hops in the car. After dinner, Shana finishes her homework and turns on the television. She watches her usual shows for a few hours, neither feeling happy or sad. This is her ritual every night until bedtime. But it didn't used to be this way.

She used to curl up with her mom on the sofa to read a story or take a bike ride around the block with her dad. But since her parents got divorced last year, Shana lives with her mom and sees her dad on the weekends. Her mom is usually tired after work, so Shana learned not to ask her to play or read to her anymore. She misses the way her family used to be.

It would be hard to name another change that has more deeply affected the nature of our society today than divorce. The proportion of one-parent households increased ten percentage points between 1970 and 2012, from 17 percent to 27 percent, according to US census statistics.[1]

Because so many children are living in single-parent homes, we want to address some of the special needs of these families especially pertaining to screen time.

The single mother or father trying to meet the needs of children while at the same time maintaining a career and some semblance of a personal life knows the tensions on the home front. If this is your situation, you know all too well the time pressures, economic demands, and loneliness you and your children have experienced. You have doubts about whether you can do an adequate job of parenting. Many times, you feel overwhelmed at the thought of doing everything yourself.

When your child asks to watch more television or play a video game for another thirty minutes, that gives you uninterrupted time to answer emails, clean the kitchen, or enjoy some needed peace and quiet. The screen becomes a convenient companion, keeping your child occupied and out of trouble. Many single parents can't afford extracurricular activities, nor do they have the time or energy to drive kids all over town. Television, video games, and surfing the Internet are the easiest ways to bide the time.

side effects of screen use

In the hearts of children whose parents divorce, anger often runs deep and lingers long. Children who have lost a parent through death need time to grieve. Channeling so much energy into feelings of sorrow, anger, or insecurity may result in lower grades at school, more aggressive negative social behavior, lessened respect for all adults, and intense loneliness.

While a child is in this unstable emotional state, he often fills the void with video games, movies, virtual worlds, or online communities. Yet excessive screen time is more likely to make a child's emotional problems deepen, not subside. According to the Mayo Clinic,[2] too much screen time has been linked to:

Obesity. The more television your child watches, the greater his risk of becoming overweight. Children are not only sedentary while watching, but they are also bombarded with advertisements for junk food. In addition, kids often snack mindlessly while they watch television.

Irregular sleep. Children who watch a lot of television are more likely to have trouble falling asleep or to have an irregular sleep schedule. Lack of sleep can lead to attention problems in school, fatigue, and overeating.

Behavioral problems. Elementary students who spend more than two hours a day watching TV or using a computer are more likely to have social, emotional, and attention problems.

Impaired academic performance. Elementary students who have a television in their bedroom tend to be outperformed by peers who don't have screens in the room.

Violence. When a child is exposed to violent video games or television, he becomes desensitized to violence. As a result, children might accept violent behavior as a suitable way to deal with problems.

Less time for play. If children use their free time for computers and television, they will have less time for active, creative play.

These side effects are experienced by any child, whether from a single-parent home or a two-parent home, but you can see how these side effects are especially detrimental for the child already struggling with behavioral and emotional problems.

The answer for children in single-parent families is not additional screen time. Children overwhelmed with negative feelings already have a hard time thinking clearly. Reading together is a positive solution that can help your children begin to think clearly about their pain and loss. You will want to select stories appropriate to the ages of your children, through the early teen years. This can be a warm, bonding time between you. Be alert to your child's reactions as you read to her. To open opportunities for discussion at her level, ask what she is thinking. Making up stories together will give you a glimpse of what is going on inside your children, at levels they may be unable to articulate in discussion.

reducing screen time, protecting me time

Most single parents are working full time to support the family and are physically exhausted by the end of the day. There's no question that a single parent will struggle with having enough energy to handle all the responsibilities of work and home. Yet it's important that parents don't succumb to nonstop television, video games, and screen time just because they are too tired to engage with their children.

How does a single parent reduce screen time for a child while still protecting the "me time" she desperately needs? One of the best things is to set an early bedtime for the children, particularly for younger children. When you put your child to bed early, he learns to adjust to that routine. If your child isn't ready to fall asleep that early, you can say, "You don't have to go to sleep right away, but you have to go to your room and be quiet. You can read a book for a few minutes until you go to sleep." This allows the single parent some time at the end of the day to be alone, to breathe deeply, and to do the things that need to be done around the home without interruptions.

An early bedtime is a good idea for children in single-parent and two-parent homes. My (Gary) grandkids, who are ten and fourteen, routinely go to bed at 8:00 p.m. They can read in their rooms before going to sleep, but they know at 8:00 p.m., it's time to settle down. Children do what they are trained to do. When a single parent trains his children to go to bed early, it gives that parent the time he desperately needs to take care of himself, while providing healthy sleep for the children.

Single parents must also evaluate how much time each day is devoted to screen time. Studies show that children who live in homes with a single mother are spending more time in front of a screen on a daily basis.[3] If your child is watching television or playing video games for more than two hours, work on a plan to reduce his or her screen time. You might begin with these simple action steps:

Decide in advance what programs your child can watch. Wait until the show is on before turning on the television.

Turn off the television when the program is over. Don't use the TV as background noise.

Make a screen-time chart for the week. Mark how much screen time your child has each day and have him check it off once he uses it. Decide if the time carries over if he doesn't use it.

Designate certain days of the week, like weekends, for video games or television days while the rest of the week stays media-free.

Don't allow eating in front of the TV or computer. Eventually your child will get hungry and switch gears.

Talk with your child about why you are making these screen-time adjustments. Discuss the benefits of less screen time and more playtime or reading time. Your child will probably resist at first, but eventually he will thank you for getting his screen-time use under control.

different parents, different rules

Zack is a hyper six-year-old who loves playing video games. When he is at his dad's house on the weekends, he can play as much as he wants. He and his dad play video games for hours together. But during the week at his mom's house, Zack is allowed to play games for only one hour per day.

"Mom," Zack complains, "why can't I play more like I do at Dad's house? I can't wait to go back to Dad's house."

Zack's mom has explained there are different rules at Dad's house and at her house. Naturally, she feels frustrated by her ex-husband's more lenient screen-time rules, and Zack feels frustrated because he can't have what he wants.

In one-parent homes that result from divorce, some children like Zack have ongoing contact with the noncustodial parent. Others suffer from negative contact or a total lack of relationship. When two adults are co-parenting like Zack's parents, they ideally will come together on what the screen-time rules are going to be, making them as congruent as possible for the sake of the child.

If Zack's mom prohibits video games while his dad offers unlimited game time, Zack is going to get whiplash going back and forth between those settings. But it is reasonable for Zack's mom to set limits and say something like, "At our house, we are going to play one hour a day. I can't control your father. He's your father. Obviously he is going to do whatever he thinks is best for you. But I'm your mother, and I have to do what I think is best."

Sometimes a mother and a father are antagonistic toward each other. Even then, it would be worthwhile for a single mom or dad to suggest getting together to set media guidelines that would work in both homes. You may want to get a counselor or pastor to sit down with you to help work out similar guidelines. Sometimes this will be a success, and other times no compromises will be reached because one parent is uncooperative. But it is always worth a try for the sake of your child.

The noncustodial parent is often tempted to shower a child with gifts like video games or a tablet, perhaps from the pain of separation or feelings of guilt over leaving the family. When these gifts are overly expensive, ill-chosen, and contrasted with what the custodial parent can provide, they are really a form of bribery, an attempt to buy the child's love. They may also be a subconscious way of getting back at the custodial parent.

If a child has conservative screen limits with Mom but a generous allowance of screen time with Dad, a child will prefer going to the home where the fun is. After spending a weekend with new toys, movies, and unlimited video games, being home with the custodial parent during the week is a drag. A child can display anger at the stricter parent, but in time will realize it was the stricter parent who truly cared. As children get older, they often recognize that their noncustodial parent was using gifts and being overly permissive to manipulate them and earn their favor.

When a divorced couple can work together to raise their children with similar values and media guidelines, the children respond well. While it is still uncommon for divorced people to work together in this way for the good of their children, more parents are attempting to do so.

Screen-Smart Single Dad: Jake's Story

Jake is a single dad of two energetic boys, Landon, age seven, and Dylan, age nine. A few years ago, Jake's wife died in a tragic car accident. The family is adjusting to this new normal with the help of extended family and friends. For the boys, summer means traveling out-of-state to visit Grandma for two months.

At Grandma's, the boys are allowed to watch hours of television and play video games as much as they want during their free time, something they are not allowed to do at home. The boys went to summer camps and had plenty of outdoor activities, but they were spending up to five hours a day in front of a screen.

When they got home from the summer at Grandma's, Landon and Dylan were glued to the television. Jake thought, "No way. My kids are not going to be glued to screens after school."

He announced a bold plan to his boys. "For one month, we are not going to watch television, movies, or video games. When the month is complete, we'll celebrate by going to an amusement park."

The boys didn't complain at first because they wanted to go to the amusement park. Instead of watching television after school, the boys read books. Imagine Jake's delight when he found his boys glued to books instead of the tube. Some mornings, Jake would even find the kids awake at 6:00 a.m. reading.

After a few weeks, Dylan said, "I'm glad we're doing this because books are a lot better than television." Of course, the month had its difficulties too, like when Jake wanted to watch the football game or take the boys to a new movie on a weekend and couldn't. But for the most part, the monthlong media fast was a breath of fresh air and elevated reading in their home.

When the month ended, however, the boys quickly went back to their television watching. "It's so easy to go back," admitted Jake. The boys have daily limits of watching one hour in the morning before school and one hour after school. They can also earn bonus points if they don't watch television on weekdays, and those bonus points translate into earning more allowance.

"Television is loud and distracting," said Jake. "If you want to talk to someone, you have to compete with the television. Without TV, kids find better things to do. They'll draw or read, write stories, or talk to each other."

Jake has this advice for single parents: "Don't use television as a crutch. Your kids can have books, games, or toys, and they will gravitate to these other things. Your kids may complain, but just say, 'Sorry, we're not turning on the TV.' They may throw a tantrum for a week, but they'll adjust. You have to be willing to invest in them."

filling your child's tank even when yours is empty

Filling your son's or daughter's love tank can seem impossible at times. You are exhausted, your child is demanding, and you may feel that you need love yourself. Yet no matter how challenging the situation, you can take small steps each day to show love to your children, particularly by speaking your child's primary love language. The needs of children in single-parent homes are the same as of children from two-parent homes. It is the *way* these needs are met that changes; one parent is the primary caregiver instead of two. And the caregiver, whether single through divorce, death, or never being married, is usually wounded.

The children are also hurting. The most common emotions are fear, anger, and anxiety. Movies, television, video games, and virtual worlds rarely bring healing in these areas. It's more likely that excessive or inappropriate screen time will magnify these negative emotions. Negative emotions can readily drain love from a child's emotional tank. Denial, anger, then bargaining, and more anger are common responses to grief, which is felt by children of divorce and by those who have experienced the death of a parent. Some children can move through these stages of grieving more quickly if significant adults in their lives seek to openly communicate with them about their loss. They need someone to talk with and cry with.

Unfortunately, screen time prevents this deep communication from happening and can delay children's healing processes because they never take the time to grieve. Digital distractions delay the pain, and years later those feelings of fear, anger, and anxiety frequently surface. Listening much, talking less, helping your child face reality, acknowledging hurt, and empathizing with pain is all a part of the healing process. But these things cannot happen via text or instant messaging.

If you are aware of your child's primary love language, your efforts to meet his emotional needs will be more effective. For instance, Robbie's love language was physical touch. His father left when he was nine years old. Looking back, Robbie says, "If it had not been for my granddaddy, I'm not sure I would have made it. The first time I saw him after my father left, he took me in his arms and held me for a long time. He didn't say anything, but I knew he loved me and would always be there for me. Every time he came to see me, he hugged me, and when he left, he did the same thing. I don't know if he knew how much the hugs meant, but they were like rain in the desert for me.

"My mom helped a lot by letting me talk and by asking questions and encouraging me to share my pain. I knew she loved me, but in the early stages, I wasn't willing to receive her love," Robbie admitted. "She would try to hug me, and I'd push her away. I think I blamed her for my father leaving. It wasn't until I found out that he left for another woman that I realized how I had misjudged her. Then I started receiving her hugs, and we became close again."

Learning to fill your child's love tank while your own is running low may seem difficult. But, like Robbie's mother, the wise parent will come to understand what her child uniquely needs—and seek to meet that need.

If you've ever flown in an airplane, you've heard the flight attendant instruct you to put on your own oxygen mask before assisting your child with their oxygen mask in case of emergency. Don't discount your own emotional need for love because it is just as real as your child's need. Because that need can no longer be met by a former spouse or by a child, the single parent must learn to reach out to friends and family members for support.

finding community

No parent can single-handedly meet a child's need for love. This is where grandparents and other extended family members, as well as church and community resources, come into play. Extended family members are always important, but they become even more crucial when children suffer losses or when life is unstable. Nearby grandparents can help the grandchildren during the school week, and their presence can cheer their own single-parent son or daughter. They take some of the emotional burden off the single parent.

Of course, this is not always possible. Your nearest family member may be hundreds of miles away. If you are a single parent, don't wait until people ask if they can help. Some may be holding back, not wanting to interfere in your family. Others may not be aware of your situation. If you or your children need help, you may want to investigate the resources available in your community. Someone at your child's school or your church may be able to guide you in your search. The more exposure your children have to positive role models, the better.

Being a single parent is one of the toughest assignments out there. Alice, who has been divorced for several years, depended on her son for love and acceptance. She poured her life into him and never crossed him because she feared his disapproval. As her son grew into a teenager, he became consumed with video games, and Alice never corrected him even when his schoolwork suffered. She needed her son to like her because it gave her the love and acceptance she desperately needed.

Single parents must have strong friendships outside of the home so they are not dependent on their children to meet their emotional needs. Although a single parent can connect with friends online through social networking, fulfilling relationships need to be nurtured face to face or voice to voice over the telephone. Too many adults are relying on texts and tweets to stay connected to others, and it's simply not enough. Many single moms spend hours on sites like Pinterest or Facebook and never really connect with anyone in a meaningful way.

Here's one word of caution about making new friends: the single parent is extremely vulnerable to members of the opposite sex who may take advantage in a time of weakness. Because the single parent so desperately needs love, there is a danger of accepting that love from someone who will take advantage sexually, financially, or emotionally. So be selective in making new friends. The safest source of love and community is from long-term friends who know members of your extended family. A single parent who tries to satisfy the need for love and community in an irresponsible manner can end up with heartache upon heartache.

As a parent, you have the greatest influence in your child's life. The way you handle your singleness with dignity and wisdom can be a source of tremendous strength for your child. You can help restore your child's sense of security, not by the companionship of screens but with your companionship and the friendship of others. When you build a community of people who care about you and your children, your child will adjust well to life in the real world instead of retreating to a screen world. Your child may not reach the next level on the latest video game, but he will reach succeeding emotional levels, with you leading the way by your example.

> *"I believe the most damaging effect of the digital world is the parent's own dependence on digital media because it will become their child's dependence."*
> —ANONYMOUS PASTOR FOR COLLEGE-AGE STUDENTS[1]

chapter fourteen

screen time and
you

Russell, a father of three, works as an independent contractor and is constantly on his phone. There are jobs to check on and future business to secure. Russell also volunteers at his church, heading up the men's ministry. He plans weekend barbeques, service project days, and breakfast meetings. He does a great job keeping men informed of upcoming events by calling and texting, but to his kids Russell seems forever occupied with his phone.

Russell's wife, Nancy, isn't faring much better. Her kids and Russell's friends call her the "Twitter Queen," and that isn't meant as a compliment. Nancy scans through her tweets incessantly and posts several times a day. On date nights, she sits with Russell at dinner with phone in hand, replying to tweets and tweeting about her menu choices. Her constant connection to social media is driving Russell crazy, but he doesn't want to nag.

Nancy is also involved in women's ministry. Her dependence on social media began quite innocently. She would notice someone in need and send an encouraging tweet during the week. The recipient of the tweet was so touched that Nancy began sending messages to more women in the church to encourage them. Before she knew it, she was constantly communicating with friends on social media. Being digitally connected became a part of her life, and she didn't know how to stop.

Russell and Nancy aren't the only parents having trouble balancing their screen time and family time. Parents are glued to their phones while they walk their kids from the parking lot to the school yard. At home, moms and dads constantly face screens, whether it's a computer, tablet, television, or phone. We're busy checking emails, social media, stock prices, daily news, and text messages. Headlines grab our attention while our kids go unnoticed.

No child wants to compete with screens for their parents' attention, nor should a child have to. Yet adults are becoming increasingly dependent on their devices, eroding communication with their children. Kids don't need constant attention from their parents, but they do need the assurance that they rank above the noise of the screen world.

growing up just like you

Children learn from imitating parents from the very start. Professors Andrew Meltzoff and Patricia Kuhl from the University of Washington show videos of babies at forty-two minutes old, already imitating adults. When the adult stuck his tongue out, the baby did the same. Not even one hour old, and the babies mirrored the adults' behavior.[2] When you became a parent, you quickly realized that baby was counting on you for protection and direction. Now that your baby has grown into a child, he needs you to be digitally wise because chances are he is going to grow up to imitate your example.

Young children watch where a parent focuses attention and will follow a mother's gaze. When parents exhibit a fascination with phones, tablets, or computers, children naturally will be curious about those things too. If the phone is the central focus of a parent's attention, a toddler is going to think, "I need to play with *that!*" It's not so much that the toddler is fascinated with the phone itself; he is first fascinated with whatever his mother finds fascinating.

What we *model* digitally is more important than what we *say* about screen time. If we as parents are totally consumed all our waking hours with electronic media of any kind, we are communicating, "This is what life is about. This is the norm." Too often parents give the right message but in the wrong manner. We tell our children to limit screen time, but then we spend hours online after work. We say social media is unhealthy, but we've got Facebook running in the background. We say video games are a waste of time and then spend two hours after work unwinding with a game. As one child said, "My parents say I waste a lot of time with my iPad, but I see them doing exactly the same thing."

It seems unfair to a child when he is expected to do something his parent hasn't been able to do. As the late Howard Hendricks said so well, "You cannot impart what you do not possess."[3] The most effective teaching takes place when a parent shows a child how to manage the digital world wisely out of his own positive experience with technology. If your digital role model isn't quite ready to be imitated by your children, it may be time for you to take a break yourself, to learn firsthand that it's okay to be unavailable in an overly wired world.

step away from the phone

It doesn't matter if you're a stay-at-home mom or an ad executive. The temptation to constantly use screens is all around you. Smartphones and tablets are portable, right by your side throughout the day. The screen world is enticing, promising something new with every interaction. *Beep. Someone messaged you.* Of course, you immediately check your phone because you want to know if it's urgent or important. It's neither, but you have been trained to respond at a moment's notice.

Often screen time leads to something pleasurable like an email bearing good news or a funny photo. A squirt of dopamine is released, and this intermittent reward keeps you coming back for more. It doesn't matter if it's a text saying thank you or a great deal on shoes; the gratification that comes from the click is real. If you are not careful, this rush of responding to blinking lights and buzzing gadgets can be addicting.

A very small percentage of Americans, fewer than 10 percent, are clinically addicted to technology, but about 65 percent of people abuse it, according to technology addiction therapist Dr. David Greenfield.[4] "The phone's never off, so we're never off," he said. "You sleep with it next to your pillow. We're not designed to be vigilant 24-7."[5]

The wired world has moved the workplace right into the family living room. We are no longer forced to leave our work behind at an office desk; we take endless emails and problems home with us through our devices. Employers capitalize on this connectivity by expecting emails and texts to be responded to immediately, even after hours. Or maybe since we've "twittered" away our time during the workday browsing the Internet and checking personal emails, we need to get caught up at home.

Is it really that important to be plugged in 24/7 to your work? For some professions, the answer is yes. But for most, the answer is no. You are able to set boundaries regarding when you are unavailable by phone or email. Poor screen management can't be pinned on a boss. Each person must take responsibility for how he uses screens and how much time per day is devoted to technology.

For many parents, it's not a job that ties them to a phone all day. It's simply become a habit to constantly check the phone, scroll through emails, or click through channels. Friends have come to expect instant responses to texts and social media posts. While we are jumping through hoops to respond to everyone else within minutes, our children are the ones on hold. They are watching and learning from our digital reliance.

The smartphone was created to make your life more convenient. If you don't answer the phone, the caller can leave a voice mail or choose to text. You don't have to reply right away. The digital information left by the caller isn't going anywhere. If you take a call or answer a text while you are talking to your children, you're setting a model for them. The phone takes precedence over talking with one another.

Of course there will be exceptions when you are anticipating an important call and you tell your family members you will need to take it whenever it comes. If you are in the middle of texting and your child wants to talk to you, it's fine to say, "Honey, let me finish this text." After finishing the text, don't move on to something else without checking back with your child. Give her your undivided attention, face to face, for those few seconds as she asks a question or makes a comment. That short, focused, positive interaction communicates, "You are important to me," particularly to the child whose primary love language is quality time.

Some young adults who are

Cellphones by the Numbers

According to the Pew Internet Project's research:[6]

91 percent of American adults have a cellphone.

56 percent of American adults have a smartphone.

67 percent of cell owners find themselves checking their phone for messages, alerts, or calls—even when they don't notice their phone ringing or vibrating.

44 percent of cell owners have slept with their phone next to their bed because they wanted to make sure they didn't miss calls, text messages, or updates during the night.

29 percent of cell owners describe their cellphones as "something they can't imagine living without."

63 percent of cell owners use their phones to go online.

disenchanted with constant digital connection have a new game. When dining in a restaurant, they stack their phones in the middle of the table. Whoever reaches for his phone first during the meal has to pay the tab for the table. Another practice gaining popularity is placing all mobile devices in a special box during mealtimes at home in order to give the present of presence. Still others have been ditching their phones in a container at the front door, much like you would an umbrella. Stepping away from your phone for the sake of your family is a healthy idea, no matter how you want to play that out in your own home.

digital sabbath and spaces

When my (Arlene's) husband and I were married more than fifteen years ago, he had a strange request. Could we have a TV-free home for the first month of our marriage? He wanted to spend quality time together in the evenings after work instead of turning on the tube. Although it was quite a stretch (I was working as a television producer then), we did it. When we brought the television back, it seemed like a noisy intruder to our peaceful oasis. We've never subscribed to cable or watched TV in our home since.

As a result, our children (ages four, seven, and nine) have grown up in a TV-free home. My kids aren't up on the latest programs. They've never had the television on as background noise. When it is movie night or we watch a funny video online, it's a big event and the kids come running. But I can honestly say a media-poor life has given us a family-rich life. Ethan, Noelle, and Lucy have grown up with a love of books, music, and exercise and with plenty of time for imaginative play. I am not advocating that canceling cable is for every household. But I do want to encourage you that it is possible to raise your children differently even in a media-saturated world.

My oldest, Ethan, is in fourth grade, and his friends can't believe he doesn't have a television or video games. "You poor thing, what do you do all day?" they ask. Ethan smiles and says he likes to read, play the piano, and build things with Legos. It may be difficult at first to cut back on television for your family, but in time, healthier alternatives will arise in the absence of television.

Now before you think I'm unaffected by screen time, let me confess. I may not watch television, but my home computer with its dual monitors is always humming. I'm constantly sitting in front of my computer, writing books or blogs, checking emails and social media, updating my calendar and contacts. I've explained that Mommy is an author who works from home, which legitimizes my screen time to my children. But I know many times I'm shopping on Amazon or reading a friend's blog, spending unnecessary minutes with my screens instead of taking a break.

Spouses are especially gifted at pointing out areas for improvement, and when I asked James about my screen time, he exclaimed, "You are *always* on your computer!" As a result, I am experimenting by turning off my computer after dinner. This forces me to be more productive in the daytime and ensures that I won't waste my time mindlessly online in the evening.

Most adults automatically check their devices several times an hour. Staring at screens is anything but relaxing. So when you set a curfew for all your gadgets and power off at the same time each night, it will actually prepare you to have a better night's rest. You can put yourself, not just your kids, on a schedule. How much television are *you* going to watch per day? How long are *you* going to stay online?

William Powers, author of *Hamlet's BlackBerry: A Practical Philosophy for Building a Good Life in the Digital Age*, decided to try a simple experiment to bring back the notion of a refreshing weekend. They created their own digital Sabbath by unplugging their home modem from Friday at bedtime until Monday morning. At first, it was incredibly hard for Powers, his wife, and son. They saw how badly they needed digital connection when they saw how hooked they were. After two months of dark computer screens, it started to get easier. After four or five months, they began to actually enjoy the benefits.

"We'd peeled our minds away from the screens where they'd been stuck. We were really there with one another and nobody else, and we could all feel it," writes Powers. "There was an atmospheric change in our minds, a shift to a slower, less restless, more relaxed way of thinking. We could just *be* in one place, doing one particular thing, and enjoy it. . . . The digital medium allows everything to be stored for later use. It was still out there; it was just a little further away. The notion that we could put the crowd, and the crowded part of our life, at a distance like this was empowering in a subtle but significant way. It was a reminder that it was ours to put at a distance."[7]

I (Gary) posted a question on my Facebook page about how to create more distance between ourselves and our digital devices. Here are a few of the responses:

- We are putting a bin at our front door with a sign that says, "Unless you are expecting a call from God, the pope, or the president, please deposit your device here so we can make the most of our time together."
- We unplug from the time we get home until we get up again the next morning.
- Try going without devices in your home just two days a week and see how relaxed and refreshed you are. Enjoy the outdoors the other days. True happiness!
- Wireless is on a timer so it goes off at night.

There are many ways you can tailor-make a digital Sabbath that will work well for you and your family. As you pull away from the noise of the screen, you will be able to tune into the hearts of your children more easily.

rules for parents

In an advice column in the *Wall Street Journal,* one parent asked:

> Dear Dan,
> I waste about two hours each day playing stupid games on my iPhone. It feels so innocent, but it actually makes me lose focus at work and takes up time I should be spending with my wife and kids. Do you have an idea for how I can ditch this bad habit?

Here is the answer from columnist Dan Ariely:

> One way to fight bad habits is to create rules. When you start a diet, for example, you can set yourself a rule such as "I won't drink sugary beverages." But to be effective, rules need to be clear and well defined . . . In your case, you could decide that, from now on you won't be playing the iPhone between 6 a.m. and 9 p.m. And to help you follow this rule, you should let your loved ones know. Or you could set up game bans for weekdays or working hours. Good luck.[8]

Digital rules aren't only good for kids; they are great for parents too. Be specific when you create rules about time limits, content allowed, and what you make exceptions for. We understand it's not easy to implement new rules. In fact, since so many adults can't curb their online use alone, there are programs that actually track and report digital activity, block distracting websites, and set alarms when users have gone over allotted times. Accountability to a spouse or friend is also effective when both parties know what to ask and report, and when they establish rewards and consequences.

Use positive language when you are creating new digital house rules for yourself. Don't put the emphasis on *disconnecting,* as if you are losing out. Instead focus on *connecting.* Think about what you will be gaining through connecting more frequently with your family and taking a break from technology. Make it a habit to put down your phone or look away from your computer when someone in the family is talking to you. Eye contact is the basis for empathy between family members. In a screen-driven world, you must fight to keep those emotional connections alive and healthy.

My (Arlene's) friend Jody, a mother of four, noticed that she needed to change the screen-time rules around her house, not only for her kids but for herself. She decided to try a "digital detox" for a few days and made these observations:

> Even after just one day, the kids were calmer and more apt to have a more thoughtful conversation with each other. The urge for Minecraft, My Little Pony, YouTube, Google, etc. was taking over their ability to be empathetic with one another. In all honesty, I found myself battling it too. I almost want to chuck my phone out the window because I'll check email, then find myself pinning ideas I'll never get to on Pinterest, or Facebook, or Instagram. It just makes me so inattentive and unproductive, which is completely opposite of what it's supposed to do. It can be such a pitfall, and I don't want my kids to remember me as unfocused.

What digital guidelines would help you personally make the most out of your screen time? Sabbath days when you take a break from screens? A cutoff time in the evening? A bin to hold your phone during mealtimes? Every person is different, so cater your plan to fit your family's schedule and priorities. But do set specific guidelines or you risk wasting precious hours online when you could be creating permanent bonds with your spouse or children.

If you are married, remember that your kids are very aware of how you and your spouse treat one another in relation to technology. Are you both preoccupied with screens, or do you talk, laugh, and cuddle together? Do you take a phone call even when you are in the middle of an important conversation? If your phone rates higher than your spouse in terms of your time and attention, there is something wrong.

Sometimes married couples don't agree on screen-time rules for themselves or their children. This is a common problem, not just regarding technology but in every area of life as well. Two people don't always agree. A husband and a wife need to listen to each other empathetically, trying to understand where the partner is coming from. Affirm each other and say, "I hear what you are saying. Can we find a meeting place in the middle?"

Maybe one of you thinks three hours is a good limit for screen time and the other thinks two hours is plenty. Then agree on two-and-a-half hours of screen time. Look for rules you both can live with and be consistent with rather than making screen-time decisions a battlefield. If you don't learn to resolve conflict within your marriage, your children are going to have a difficult time resolving conflict in the future. It's extremely important for children to see their parents coming together regarding screen time and other issues.

saying goodbye to the electronic babysitter

Finally, you may be ready to make personal screen-time changes, but you aren't ready to give up the electronic babysitter for your children. Neil, father of two boys ages two and four, relies on the television to entertain the boys after he gets home from work. His wife works in the evenings, and he needs some time to unwind from a busy day and to make dinner. "When the boys are in front of the television, they are quiet and calm. I must confess it's a great babysitter when you need one."

It's certainly easier to allow your children to watch hours of television than to provide alternative activities or monitor their behavior. But the easy way is not always the best way. What results can an electronic babysitter yield compared to an involved, proactive parent? What you do in the first eighteen years of your child's life is monumental in his development into an adult. Your investment as a parent will pay huge dividends in your child's life, particularly between the ages of eighteen and thirty-five.

We are empathetic to the parents who are getting by and taking the path of least resistance out of desperation. But too many families are going down the easy route of digital dependence, and the results in society will be negative. Too many teenagers are depressed, sexually active, addicted to substances, and rebellious toward authority. As a parent, you've got to purpose in your heart to fight the negative effects of screen time and electronic babysitters.

Begin with an honest inspection of how you use screen time in your own life and with your children. Parents who constantly check and use phones and tablets in the presence of their children are contributing to their children's overuse of the screen. You hold in your hand a golden opportunity to teach your child how to master their screen time—by learning to master your own.

"Youth do not think into the future far enough. There are great tomorrows we must encourage youth to dream of." —HENRIETTA C. MEARS

a tale of
two homes

Jill and Elena grew up as neighbors. Just months apart in age, they spent countless hours playing outside, riding bikes and scooters, jumping rope, and making up games. But after Jill received a tablet for her seventh birthday, she began playing video games more and coming out to play less. Within a few months, Jill seemed like a completely different girl.

Elena kept knocking on the door, but the answer was always the same. "Sorry, Jill is busy playing a game right now. Maybe she'll come out to play later." But later never came.

Although Jill's mom joked about losing her daughter to video games, inside she was concerned. She knew childhood was not supposed to look like a little girl attached to a tablet for four to five hours every day, addicted to video games. She had tried to get Jill to stop, but Jill screamed and pounded her fists on the table, demanding to have the tablet back. Her mom didn't know what to do. She didn't have the stamina to fight Jill all the time.

Across the street, Elena was limited to thirty minutes of screen time on educational websites on the weekend and two weeknights when she didn't have soccer practice. Elena found other children in the neighborhood to play with. She was easygoing and made new friends readily, although she missed playing with Jill. Screens played a small part in Elena's life, and she couldn't understand why Jill stayed inside on weekends.

The tale of these two homes is being written right now. How will technology shape Jill and Elena as adults? These two girls from the same neighborhood are heading to very different places.

who's in charge of the castle?

My husband, James, has a particular article he loves to talk about with any father who will listen. It's a piece that ran in the *Wall Street Journal* called "A Ride in Dad's Traveling Think Tank." In the article, the author contrasts the car ride of yesterday and the car ride of today:

> In my dad's generation, a man's car was his castle. And his kids were his captive audience. We listened to his music. We answered his questions . . . Now I've got my own kids, but I don't drive a think tank. I just drive a tank. It's a minivan, but there's nothing mini about it. I call it my Maxivan, or rather, the kids call it their Maxivan. You see, they think of it as their car, not mine. And they're not wrong.[1]

James decided long ago he didn't want to be trapped in his minivan with kids' cartoons and endless songs that rhymed. He was going to take back his car. Children's music was summarily replaced with conversations and audiobook biographies. The family van was transformed into a university on wheels, with Dad reigning as king of the castle once more. Whether or not you listen to educational material is not the point. The point is that you can listen to whatever you choose because it's *your* car, not your child's. It's time to take back your car, which is connected to taking back your home from the technology you don't want.

You are the parent at the wheel who decides the direction of your family. If you take the path less traveled, you're going against the grain in this screen-driven world. Your child may not have a cellphone when her contemporaries do. Your son may not know how to play the video game everyone's talking about. Pop culture references may go right over your daughter's head.

But what might your child gain by minimizing the impact of screens on his life? Freedom from addiction, strong family relationships, empathy, critical reasoning, and patience come to mind. The superhighway of screen entertainment may be more popular and convenient, but screen time isn't producing the character and quality relationships most parents desire for their children.

When my (Gary's) children were growing up, we set a guideline of no more than thirty minutes a day of television. That was a long time ago, and screens weren't nearly as prevalent in the home. But setting that time limit for television was critical because my children could have watched hours every day if my wife, Karolyn, and I didn't have a plan.

The same principles that guided our home decades ago still hold true today. The close-knit family of yesteryear can be your reality in this present digital age. When you have a purpose and a plan, screen time can be a wonderful way to bring your family closer. But left as a default activity, technology will rob your family of quality time and shared memories every time.

So what kind of home will you create? A home centered around screens or a home centered around people? When you have the latter, you will be drastically different from the average screen-driven home. Your home will be like a castle on a hill, providing light not only to your children but also to your world.

notes

introduction

1. Douglas Gentile and David Walsh, *A Normative Study of Family Media Habits* (Minneapolis: National Institute on Media and the Family, 2002), quoted in ParentFurther, "E-Parenting: Media and Advertising," www.parentfurther.com.
2. Andy Andrews, *The Noticer* (Nashville: Thomas Nelson, 2011, *111*).

chapter one: screen time: too much, too soon?

1. American Academy of Pediatrics, "Policy Statement: Media Use by Children Younger than 2 Years," *American Academy of Pediatrics* (2011) http://pediatrics.aappublications.org.
2. K. Nelson, "Structure and Strategy in Learning to Talk," *Monographs of the Society for Research in Child Development*, 38, no. 1–2 (1973): 1–35; and D. L. Linebarger and D. Walker, "Infants' and Toddlers' Television Viewing and Language Outcomes," *American Behavioral Scientist*, 48, no. 5 (2005): 624–45.
3. F. J. Zimmerman, D. A. Christakis, and A. N. Meltzoff, "Television and DV/Video Viewing in Children Younger than 2 Years," *Archives of Pediatric and Adolescent Medicine*, 161, no. 5 (2007): 473–79.
4. E. A. Vandewater et al., "When the Television Is Always On," *American Behavioral Scientist*, 48, no. 5 (2005): 562–77.
5. M. E. Schmidt et al., "The Effects of Background Television on the Toy Play Behavior of Very Young Children," *Child Development*, 79, no. 4 (2008): 1137–51.
6. V. J. Rideout and E. Hamel, *The Media Family: Electronic Media in the Lives of Infants, Toddlers, Preschoolers, and Their Parents* (Menlo Park, CA: Kaiser Family Foundation, 2006).
7. V. J. Rideout, U. G. Foehr, and D. F. Roberts, "Generation M2: Media in the Lives of 8- to 18-Year-Olds," Henry J. Kaiser Family Foundation, January 20, 2010, http://kff.org.
8. "Too Much 'Screen Time' for Kids Could Cause Long-Term Brain Damage, Warn Experts," *Huffington Post UK*, May 22, 2012, www.huffingtonpost.co.uk.

9. American Heart Association, "Many Teens Spend 30 Hours a Week on 'Screen Time' during High School," *Science Daily,* March 14, 2008, www.sciencedaily.com.

10. Dr. Kathy Koch, "Parenting Tech-Savvy Children: Negative Effects of Digital Technology," Hearts at Home conference, 2013.

11. American Academy of Pediatrics, "Media and Children," policy statement, www.aap.org.

12. A. O. Scott and Manohla Dargis, "Big Bang Theories: Violence on Screen," *New York Times,* February 28, 2013, www.nytimes.com.

chapter two: the A+ method for relational kids

1. National Center for Biotechnology Information, U.S. National Library of Medicine, research date January 1, 2014, quoted in "Attention Span Statistics," Statistic Brain.com.

chapter three: the A+ skill of affection

1. Mary Bellis, "The Invention of Television," About.com Inventors, www.inventors.about.com.

2. V. J. Rideout and E. Hamel, *The Media Family: Electronic Media in the Lives of Infants, Toddlers, Preschoolers, and Their Parents* (Menlo Park, CA: Kaiser Family Foundation, 2006).

3. Shane Hipps, *Flickering Pixels* (Grand Rapids: Zondervan, 2009), 183.

4. Gwenn Schurgin O'Keefe and Kathleen Clarke-Pearson for the American Academy of Pediatrics, "The Impact of Social Media on Children, Adolescents, and Families," *Pediatrics Digest,* March 28, 2011, www.pediatricsdigest.mobi/content.

5. Diane Swanbrow, "Empathy: College Students Don't Have as Much as They Used To," *MichiganNews,* University of Michigan, May 27, 2010, http://ns.umich.edu.

6. The American Academy of Pediatrics, "Media Education," *Pediatrics,* September 27, 2010, http://pediatrics.aapublications.org.

7. Anita Chandra et al., for the American Academy of Pediatrics, "Does Watching Sex on Television Predict Teen Pregnancy?" *Pediatrics Digest,* November 1, 2008, http://pediatrics.aapublications.org.

8. The National Campaign to Prevent Teen and Unplanned Pregnancy, *Sex and Tech: What's Really Going On* (Washington, DC: National Campaign to Prevent Teen and Unplanned Pregnancy, 2013), www.thenationalcampaign.org.

9. Jocelyn Green, email interview, September 4, 2013.

chapter four: the A+ skill of appreciation

1. Shawn Achor, *The Happiness Advantage* (New York: Crown Business, 2010), 7.

2. Melinda Beck, "Thank You. No, Thank You: Grateful People Are Happier, Healthier Long after the Leftovers Are Gobbled Up," *Wall Street Journal*, November 23, 2010, http://online.wsj.com.

3. C. Nathan DeWall et al., "A Grateful Heart Is a Nonviolent Heart: Cross-Sectional, Experience Sampling, Longitudinal, and Experimental Evidence," *Social Psychological & Personality Science* vol. 3, no. 2, March 2012, 232–40, http://spp.sagepub.com.

4. Eun Kyung Kim, "Teen Uses Tweets to Compliment His Classmates," *Today News,* January 8, 2013, www.today.com.

chapter five: the A+ skill of anger management

1. American Academy of Pediatrics Council on Communications and Media, "Policy Statement: Media Education," *Pediatrics,* November 1, 2010, http://pediatrics.apublications.org.

2. M. E. Hamburger et al., *Measuring Bullying Victimization, Perpetration, and Bystander Experiences: A Compendium of Assessment Tools* (Atlanta: Centers for Disease Control and Prevention, National Center for Injury Prevention and Control, 2011), www.cdc.gov.

chapter six: the A+ skill of apology

1. This chapter is based on *When Sorry Isn't Enough* by Gary Chapman and Jennifer Thomas (Chicago: Moody, 2013). This book is an update of the authors' *The Five Languages of Apology.*

chapter seven: the A+ skill of attention

1. Statistic Brain, "Attention Span Statistics," January 1, 2014, www.statistics-brain.com.

2. Nicholas Carr, *The Shallows: What the Internet Is Doing to Our Brains* (New York: W. W. Norton, 2011), 87.
3. Kendra Cherry, "What's the Best Predictor of School Success?" About.com Psychology, March 2, 2009, http://psychology.about.com.
4. Kathryn Zickuhr, "In a Digital Age, Parents Value Printed Books for Their Kids," *Pew Internet & American Life Project*, May 28, 2013, http://libraries.pewinternet.org.
5. Carr, *The Shallows*, 116.
6. Rutherford Elementary School, "Reading at Home," February 11, 2014, http://rutherford.jefferson.kyschools.us.
7. American Academy of Pediatrics, "Video Games Linked to Attention Problems in Children," press release, July 5, 2010, www.aap.org.
8. Bob Sullivan and Hugh Thompson, "Brain Interrupted," *New York Times,* May 3, 2013, www.nytimes.com.
9. Christine Rosen, "The Myth of Multitasking," *New Atlantis,* spring 2008, www.thenewatlantis.com.
10. Ibid.
11. Ibid.
12. Statistic Brain. "Attention Span Statistics," January 1, 2014, www.statisticsbrain.com.
13. Bob Sullivan and Hugh Thompson, "Brain Interrupted," *New York Times,* May 3, 2013, www.nytimes.com.
14. Kenneth R. Ginsburg et al., for the American Academy of Pediatrics, "The Importance of Play in Promoting Healthy Child Development and Maintaining Strong Parent-Child Bonds," *Pediatrics,* January 1, 2007, http://pediatrics.aappublications.org.
15. Carr, *The Shallows*, 219.

chapter eight: screen time and shyness

1. M. Burstein et al., "Shyness versus Social Phobia in U.S. Youth," *Pediatrics,* November 2011, www.ncbi.nlm.nih.gov.
2. Mayo Clinic, "Children and TV: Limiting Your Child's Screen Time," Mayo Clinic E-Newsletter, August 16, 2013, www.mayoclinic.org.
3. Marla E. Eisenberg et al. "Correlations between Family Meals and Psychosocial Well-being among Adolescents, *JAMA Pediatrics,* August 2004, http://archpedi.jamanetwork.com.

4. Centers for Disease Control and Prevention, "Childhood Obesity Facts," July 10, 2013, www.cdc.gov.

5. Sue Hubbard, MD, "Kids, Media, and Obesity: Too Much 'Screen Time' Can Harm Your Child's Health," *Chicago Tribune,* September 30, 2013, www.chicagotribune.com.

chapter nine: screen time and the brain

1. Kurt W. Fischer, William T. Greenough, Daniel Siegel, and Paul Thompson, "Inside the Teenage Brain," *Frontline,* WTTW: Chicago, 2002, www.pbs.org.

2. John Bruer, Mary Carskadon, and Ellen Galinsky, "Inside the Teenage Brain," *Frontline,* WTTW: Chicago, 2002, www.pbs.org.

3. Nicholas Carr, *The Shallows: What the Internet Is Doing to Our Brains* (New York: W. W. Norton), 121.

4. Matt Richtel, "Silicon Valley School Sticks to Basics, Shuns High-Tech Tools," *New York Times,* October 23, 2011, www.boston.com.

5. Eun Kyung Kim, "Bill Gates: My Kids Get Cell Phone at Age 13," *Today News,* January 30, 2013.

6. Dr. Archibald D. Hart and Dr. Sylvia Hart Frejd, *The Digital Invasion: How Technology Is Shaping You and Your Relationships* (Grand Rapids: Baker, 2013), 60.

7. Carr, *The Shallows,* 51.

8. Ibid., 77.

9. Chelsea Clinton and James P. Steyer, "Is the Internet Hurting Chilren?" *CNN Opinion,* May 21, 2012, www.cnn.com.

10. Hart and Frejd, *The Digital Invasion,* 63.

11. Jenn Savedge, "Is Your Child Addicted to Screens?" Mother Nature Network, August 12, 2013, www.thestar.com.

12. BBC News, "S. Korean Dies after Games Session" August 10, 2005, http://news.bbc.co.uk.

13. Hart and Frejd, *The Digital Invasion,* 124.

14. Kayt Sukel, "Playing Video Games May Make Specific Changes to the Brain," Dana Foundation News, January 9, 2012, www.dana.org.

15. Carr, *The Shallows,* 32.

16. Hart and Frejd, *The Digital Invasion,* 65.

17. R. Morgan Griffin, "Your Kid's Brain on Exercise," WebMD, May 8, 2013, www.webmd.com.

18. Benjamin Carson, Brainyquote.com.

chapter eleven: screen time and security

1. Nanci Hellmich, "Death of a Florida Girl Is a Wake-up Call for Parents," *USA Today*, October 16, 2013, www.usatoday.com.

2. i-SAFE, "Cyber Bullying: Statistics and Tips," 2004 data, www.isafe.org.

3. Peter Brust et al., "Growing Up Online," *Frontline*, January 22, 2008, www.pbs.org.

4. Ibid.

5. Ibid.

6. Britney Fitzgerald, "Facebook Age Requirement," *Huffington Post*, November 30, 2012.

7. Daily Infographic, "The Stats on Internet Pornography," January 4, 2013, http://dailyinfographic.com.

8. V. J. Rideout, U. G. Foehr, and D. F. Roberts, "Generation M2: Media in the Lives of 8- to 18-Year-Olds," Henry J. Kaiser Family Foundation, January 20, 2010, http://kff.org.

chapter twelve: screen time and parental authority

1. Dan Kloeffler and Nick Poppy, "Bill Cosby: 'I Wanted to Take the House Back' from Kids," *Newsmakers*, June 15, 2013, http://news.yahoo.com.

chapter thirteen: screen time and the single parent

1. Jonathan Vespa et al. "America's Families and Living Arrangements: 2012," August 2013, www.census.gov.

2. Mayo Clinic, "Children and TV: Limiting Your Child's Screen Time," August 16, 2013, www.mayoclinic.com.

3. V. J. Rideout and E. Hamel, *The Media Family: Electronic Media in the Lives of Infants, Toddlers, Preschoolers, and Their Parents* (Menlo Park, CA: Kaiser Family Foundation, 2006).

chapter fourteen: screen time and you

1. College pastor, quoted by Archibald Hart and Sylvia Hart Freud, *Digital Invasion* (Grand Rapids: Baker, 2013), 30.
2. James Fallows, "Linda Stone on Maintaining Focus in a Maddeningly Distractive World," *Atlantic*, May 23, 2013, www.theatlantic.com.
3. Dallas Theological Seminary, "Howard Hendricks Tribute," February 2013, www.dts.edu.
4. Beth Teitell, "Dad, Can You Put Away the Laptop?" *Boston Globe*, March 8, 2012, www.boston.com.
5. Beth Kassab, "Are You Addicted to Your Smartphone?" *Orlando Sentinel,* November 25, 2013, http://articles.orlandosentinel.com.
6. Pew Research, "Mobile Technology Fact Sheet," Pew Research Internet Project, December 27, 2013.
7. William Powers, *Hamlet's BlackBerry: A Practical Philosophy for Building a Good Life in the Digital Age* (New York: Harper, 2010), 228–29, 230–31.
8. Dan Ariely, "Ask Ariely: On Pointless Gaming, Topics and Teachers, and Getting Over It," *Wall Street Journal*, November 23, 2013, http://danariely.com.

conclusion: a tale of two homes

1. Dan Zevin, "A Ride in Dad's Traveling Think Tank," *Wall Street Journal*, July 16, 2012.

social development by
ages and stages

Toddlers

Speaks in complete sentences of three to five words

Follows simple directions

Enjoys helping with household tasks

Does not cooperate or share well

Begins to notice other people's moods and feelings

Preschoolers

Uses a 1,500-word vocabulary

Speaks in relatively complex sentences

Takes turns, shares, and cooperates

Can express anger verbally instead of physically

Enjoys pretending and playing dress up

Mimics adults and seeks praise

Friends become more important

Elementary School: Kindergarten–Third Grade

Becomes aware of personal emotions and can empathize with others

Uses face-to-face interactions to understand what others are feeling

Able to read nonverbal cues

More cooperative and affectionate

Curious about others and eager to make friends

Can differentiate between needs and wants

Family-oriented

Seeks parental/adult approval

Elementary School: Fourth–Sixth Grade

Chooses to play with other children of the same gender

More prone to moodiness

Influenced by peers

Loyal to groups and clubs

Enjoys using code languages

Developing decision-making skills

Needs involvement with caring adults

Quiz: does your child have
too much screen time?

These simple questions can help determine whether or not screen time is harming your child's overall health. Give a score to each question using the following ratings:

0 = Never or rarely true

1 = Occasionally true

2 = Usually true

3 = Always true

_____ Your child is upset when you ask him to stop his screen activity to come to dinner or another activity.

_____ Your child asks you to buy a digital device such as an iPod after you have already said no.

_____ Your child has trouble completing his homework because he is busy watching television or playing video games.

_____ Your child refuses to help with chores around the house, choosing instead to play with screens.

_____ Your child asks to play a video game or other screen-related activity after you have said no.

_____ Your child does not get sixty minutes of physical activity each day.

_____ Your child does not give frequent eye contact to others in the home.

_____ Your child would rather play video games than go outside to play with friends.

_____ Your child doesn't really enjoy anything that does not involve screens.

_____ If you restricted all screen use for one day, your child would be irritable and whiny.

If your child scores:

10 or below: Your child does not appear to have too much screen time. He seems able to exercise appropriate control and boundaries.

11–20: Your child may be depending on screen time too much. You will want to monitor screen time more judiciously and watch for growing reliance upon screens.

21–30: Your child may be addicted to screens. You may want to meet with a counselor, pastor, or parent you respect for advice.

Look for these and many other helpful resources at **www.5lovelanguages.com.**

Drills for Grown-Up Social Success, six interactive scenarios to help you build your child's confidence in courtesies and social interaction.

25 Common Courtesies for Kids, a quick list to help you shape goals and expectations for your child's behavior.

The Love Languages Mystery Game to help you determine your child's primary love language.

50 Table Talk Questions for Your Family, a guide to fresh and lively conversations at family mealtimes.

discussion group
questions

introduction: taking back your home

1. Is technology bringing your family closer together or driving it farther apart?
2. What do you hope to learn from reading this book?
3. What concerns regarding screen time do you have for your child?
4. Talk about the difference between good intentions and action.

chapter one: screen time: too much, too soon?

1. How did you spend your free time as a child?
2. How old are your children, and how much screen time do they have on an average day? What are they doing/watching on screens?
3. What do you think about your child having a television in his or her room?
4. What are some activities you have successfully substituted for screen time?
5. How do you respond to this statistic: "The average American child age eight to eighteen spends more than seven hours a day looking at a video game, computer, cellphone, or television"?
6. Do you currently have media guidelines for your home? If so, what are they? If not, would you like to establish guidelines as you read this book?
7. Have you met someone like Michael, the senior in high school who played video games alone during his graduation party? How does Michael's example serve as a warning?

8. How do you teach the difference between appropriate and inappropriate content to your children? Give an example of when you had to do this recently.

chapter two: the A+ method for relational kids

1. Do you agree that children in previous generations were more respectful of parents and adults? What role do you think technology has played in any changes?
2. On page 29, it says, "Technology trains (children) to find what they need at the speed of light. The art of patience is lost." Have you found this to be true with your kid(s)? If so, give an example when your child was impatient.
3. Of the five A+ skills (affection, appreciation, anger management, apology, and attention), which ones stand out as skills your child most needs to improve?
4. Talk about family mealtimes. How many times do you eat together as a family in a typical week? Is there a lot of conversation? Who is the most talkative? Do you take phone calls during meals? Is the television on? Is the meal rushed or unhurried?
5. Does your child have an email account, and if so, do you have stated email guidelines? For parents of younger children, at what age do you think it is beneficial for your child to have an email address?

chapter three: the A+ skill of affection

1. How does your child express affection toward you? How do you express affection toward your child?
2. Does your phone or computer compete with your child for your affection? How?
3. Has your child showed you and other family members less affection after receiving a digital device such as a tablet, phone, or video game?

4. Share a success story of when you were able to put aside your electronics and be "all there" for your child (or vice versa, when your child set aside his/her device to be with you).

5. What are your thoughts on screen time during playdates with friends?

6. What exposure does your child have to social media? How do you think social media can be helpful or harmful as your child seeks to be liked by others?

7. Does your child play/watch any violent video games? If so, how has that affected his/her empathy for others?

8. How does your child rate when it comes to eye contact? Does your child readily give you eye contact? Does he or she look other adults or friends in the eye?

9. How does eye contact show affection for another person?

10. What is one thing you can do to better show your child affection?

chapter four: the A+ skill of appreciation

1. Do you feel your child appreciates what you do for him or her as a parent?

2. Do you need to prompt your child to say thank you, or does he or she express thanks on his/her own?

3. Give an example of a time when you taught your child a lesson about gratitude.

4. How does it make you feel when your child receives a gift but seems ungrateful for it?

5. What is your response when your child says, "But everyone else has one!"?

6. What might be the value of making children wait for what they want instead of granting their wishes immediately?

7. Has your child said thank you in a way that touched your heart? Share that memory with the group.

8. Look at the *10 Screen-Free Ways to Cultivate a Thankful Heart in Your Child* on page 58. What is one way you would like to try with your family?

9. How has showing gratitude helped you as an adult to get along better with others?

chapter five: the A+ skill of anger management

1. Does your child have trouble managing his/her anger?

2. When your child gets angry, do you try to distract him or her with something else?

3. If your child dealt with anger in the same way you do, would you be pleased? If not, what is one thing you can do to improve your own anger management with your kid(s)?

4. Brainstorm scenarios to role-play with your children to help them practice anger management. Possible scenarios might be: What would you do if a child took away a toy you were playing with? What would you do if another kid insulted you by calling you names?

5. Think about the last time you were angry with your child or vice versa. What happened? What did you do right? What could you do differently next time?

6. Does your child have a problem with frequent outbursts of anger? What do you think is the "why" behind your child's anger?

7. Evaluate the video games your child is playing. Are there any that promote aggressive behavior?

8. Has your child ever been involved with cyberbullying?

9. Is there something you need to apologize about to your child? (You may refer to the *Helpful Dialogues for You and Your Angry Child* on page 78 as a starting point.)

chapter six: the A+ skill of apology

1. Have you modeled how to apologize to your child (either by apologizing to your child or having your child present when you are apologizing to someone else)? What happened?

2. Does your child readily accept responsibility for wrongdoing, or does he/she tend to blame someone or something else?

3. Give an example of one clear rule and consequence if that rule is broken in your home.

4. Have you ever watched one of your child's friendships weaken or break because someone wouldn't apologize? Have you ever had a similar experience?

5. In preparation for teaching your child the five languages of apology, practice role-playing with each other. Say:

   "I am sorry."

   "I was wrong."

   "What can I do to make it right?"

   "I'll try not to do it again."

   "Will you please forgive me?"

6. Agree or disagree with this statement: "I don't want to apologize to my children because they will lose respect for me." Explain your opinion.

7. Look over the *Things Not to Say When Apologizing to Your Kids* on page 92. Which of these phrases have you used in your parenting?

chapter seven: the A+ skill of attention

1. How has screen time affected your child's ability to pay attention?

2. Does your child have any difficulty paying attention in school, church, or other settings where listening is required?

3. Is your child able to sit still?

4. Have you observed your child switching back and forth between tasks instead of completing the task at hand? Give an example.

5. Talk about your child's reading habits. What's something you can do to increase your child's reading time, vocabulary, or comprehension?

6. What have you done to encourage your child to read more?

7. If your child struggles with ADHD, what are a few things you can do to help him/her navigate screen time constructively?

8. Why might multitasking be dangerous for your child?

9. Do you have any homework tips to share? (See page 106 if you need some ideas yourself).

10. How much daily play, not screen-related, is your child getting?

chapter eight: screen time and shyness

1. Just because a child is quiet does not mean he or she is shy. Consider this statement in light of your child: "When a child hears over and over that he is shy, it gives him an excuse for not developing social skills. A child can say, 'Oh, I'm just shy,' giving him a pass to skip politeness and conversation. For some children, being shy becomes very convenient."

2. If your child is playing a video game and you come home from work, does he/she pause to greet you?

3. How have you helped your child overcome anxieties about meeting new people?

4. Look over the practice scenarios on page 115. Which would you like to practice with your child?

5. What words of encouragement can you give a child struggling with shyness?

6. Has your child experienced rejection or bullying? Did you talk about it afterward?

7. Is your child a healthy weight? What's one thing you can do to promote proper nutrition and exercise?

chapter nine: screen time and the brain

1. What are you thinking when you see your child's eyes glued to the screen?

2. If your child grows up with screens throughout preschool and elementary school, how is the brain affected?

3. How does increased screen time threaten the development of skills like reading, writing, and sustained concentration?

4. What are benefits of screen time for the brain? How do those benefits measure up to the downsides?

5. If your child follows the norm, he/she will average 3,400 text messages a month as a teenager. How do you think texting will affect your child's brain in the future?

6. Do you think your child's screen time is leading to an overdose of pleasure?

7. Are you concerned that your child may become addicted to screens in the future? If so, what steps will you take to ensure his/her safety?

8. If your child's brain is plastic and being molded daily, is your child's screen time beneficial or detrimental to brain development?

9. Neurosurgeon Ben Carson said, "Don't let anyone turn you into a slave. You're a slave if you let the media tell you that sports and entertainment are more important than developing your brain." What is one positive thing you can do to develop your child's brain?

chapter ten: screen time and the love languages

1. Physical Touch: Do you make physical contact each day with your child through hugs, high fives, sitting next to each other, wrestling, etc.?

2. Words of Affirmation: When was the last time you praised your child for something specifically? What did you say?

3. Quality Time: How can you make time in your day for quality time for your child and still get your work done?

4. Gifts: Is your child preoccupied with material things? Does he/she nag you about getting an electronic device like a tablet or video game?

5. Acts of Service: What are a few caring acts of service you do regularly for your child?

6. What do you think is your child's primary love language, or his top two?

7. How can you speak in that love language to your child today?

chapter eleven: screen time and security

1. Have you had any experiences with cyberbullying online or know someone who has?

2. Talk about your plan to address pornography with your child at the appropriate age. What do you think is important to say? How can you best monitor your child's devices?

3. Have you taught your child the value of privacy and not to disclose personal facts online? How can you communicate the importance of this in a way your child understands?

4. Does your child's screen time promote learning and positive values?

5. Do you use an Internet filter, or do you plan to in the future?

6. When might be a good age for your child to get a cellphone? Describe why.

7. Have you gone over the "Screen-Safe Family Pledge" (found on page 164) with your children who are old enough to understand?

chapter twelve: screen time and parental authority

1. Do you need to "take your house back" from kids who are calling the shots and pushing your limits?

2. Do you have trouble keeping up with your child's computer use because you don't understand the programs he is using?

3. If you want your child to reduce his/her screen time, are you comfortable making those changes or are you anxious about resistance from your child?

4. Is it more important to you that your child likes you or that your child respects you?

5. Are there digital-free zones in your home (i.e., a screen-free room) or digital-free times in your schedule (i.e., devices go off for a certain time)? If so, how has that benefited your family?

6. If you have given your child too many privileges or too little supervision of screen time, what are you going to do about it now?

7. For grandparents: What are your frustrations about screen time and your grandchildren? What are standards you would like to have at your house when the children are visiting?

chapter thirteen: screen time and the single parent

1. What are some of the unique challenges you face as a single parent?

2. Does your child struggle with any of the following: obesity, irregular sleep, behavioral problems, poor academics, or violence? If yes to any, do you think screen time is a contributing factor?

3. What time does your child go to bed? Is this an early enough bedtime to make room for some quiet time for you at the end of the day?

4. Do you co-parent with an ex-spouse? Are there different screen-time rules when your child is with you and when your child is with the other parent? If so, how can you work together to provide more consistent guidelines?

5. Would you like to try a type of media fast like the dad featured on page 187? What do you think would work for you and your kids?

6. In seeking to fill your child's love tank each day, what obstacles get in the way?

7. Do you have a caring community of people who support you as a parent?

8. What are some constructive ways you can seek support from others if you don't have that right now?

chapter fourteen: screen time and you

1. Do you agree with this statement: "I believe the most damaging effect of the digital world is the parent's own dependence on digital media because it will become their child's dependence"?
2. Does your child know that spending time with him/her is more important to you than catching up on social media or answering emails?
3. Describe your digital use on a typical day. Would you be pleased if your child grew up to be just like you in terms of screen use?
4. Aside from your hours at work, are you comfortable disconnecting with technology and making yourself unavailable by phone or email during certain times?
5. If you were stranded without any digital connectivity for a week, would you be relieved, indifferent, or totally stressed?
6. When do you turn your phone off?
7. What are some positive things you have done to limit your personal screen time and enjoy more time with your family?
8. What kind of "digital Sabbath" experience would you like to create for your family?
9. Are you ready to say goodbye to the digital babysitter? How can you be more proactive as a parent and less dependent on video games and televisions shows to occupy your child?

conclusion: a tale of two homes

1. Describe your typical family car ride. Does anyone use earbuds? Are movies allowed? Is there conversation?
2. How has your thinking about screen time changed since reading this book?
3. What has stood out as important and relevant for your family?
4. What screen-time changes have you implemented or do you plan to implement?

5. Has your child resisted any changes? If so, how did you deal with it?

6. What positive outcomes for your family will be gained as you stick` to a wise media plan and enforce it?

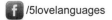 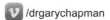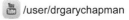

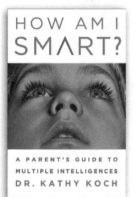
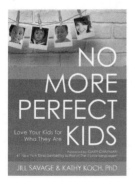

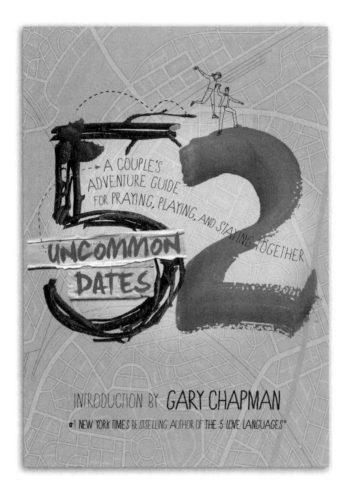

IMPROVING MILLIONS OF RELATIONSHIPS . . .

ONE LANGUAGE AT A TIME.

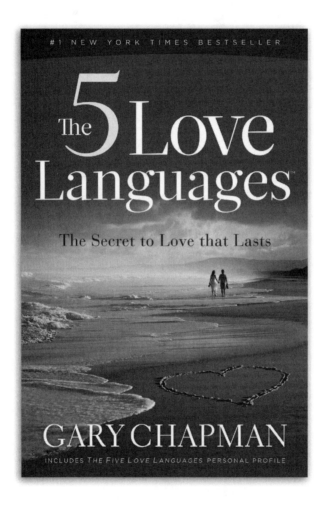

Over 9,000,000 copies sold!

"The one who chooses to love will find appropriate ways
to express that decision everyday."

—Dr. Gary Chapman

Available wherever books are sold.

building
relationships

WITH DR. GARY CHAPMAN

Get practical help for your marriage or any of your relationships. Listen to **Building Relationships**, a popular weekly Moody Radio program hosted by Dr. Gary Chapman, the *New York Times* bestselling author of *The 5 Love Languages*.

www.buildingrelationshipsradio.org